The Making of a King

by
Tom Leding

The Making of a King

by
Tom Leding

TLM Publishing
Tulsa, Oklahoma

The majority of scriptures in this book are from *The Holy Bible, New International Version* (NIV), (Grand Rapids: The Zondervan Corporation, 1990, copyright 1973, 1978, 1984 by the International Bible Society. Other scriptures are from *The King James Version of the Holy Bible* (KJV) and *The Living Bible* (TLB), (Wheaton: Tyndale House Publishers, 1971).

The Making of a King
ISBN 1-890915-03-3
Copyright 1997 by
Tom Leding
TLM Publishing
4412 S. Harvard
Tulsa, OK 74135

Contents

Foreword

I grew up in Tulsa, Oklahoma, and as a teenager, I heard a daily feature on my father's radio. Each morning, a local insurance executive would give a powerful, positive "quote for the day." After the quote, the announcer would ask, "Who said that?" The speaker would reply with his name, "Tom Leding."

Throughout my years at home and anywhere in the Tulsa region of Oklahoma, Tom Leding's "Who Said That?" program became associated with some of the greatest thoughts and ideas of all times, as he expanded his own thoughts with the wisdom of others. Many of the powerful statements from his radio broadcast have been collected in a previous book called, *Wisdom for Success in Life.* I highly recommend that book to anyone in any field.

As someone who grew up listening to Tom deliver the wisdom of the ages on his daily radio program, I was both shocked and honored when he asked me to write a foreword to this book, *The Making of a King.*

From the beginning of recorded history, various kingdoms have been birthed, risen to power, and then fallen into obscurity. Some of the monarchs won rulership through war or violence of some kind. However, many of them became rulers through virtue of their heritage, through being born into a royal bloodline.

Regardless of how they gained their thrones, some monarchs have reigned with distinction, grace, and wisdom. However, far too many rulers were not prepared to handle the awesome responsibility and were tyrants or capricious and self-centered "wimps." Nor did many of them prepare their heirs for kingship. History has shown us clearly that a kingdom or an empire is only as significant and powerful as its ruler.

In America, we are fortunate to live in a society where we can each seek his or her own level of productivity. We are not born into a caste society doomed to live out lives of degradation or mediocrity. Instead, we are given "the keys to the castle" in every area of our lives. Therefore, it is accurate to state that everyone born in the United States has "inherited" a kingdom.

The size and significance of our individual kingdoms is not determined by the greatness or wealth of our ancestors, but by each person's personal vision and ability to apply kingdom principles as outlined in this book. In addition, those born again are royalty — joint-heirs with Jesus (Rom. 8:17) — and have the responsibility to be good stewards (rulers) over the portions of God's "kingdom on earth" that their lives constitute.

We are not only to pray that God's Kingdom comes on earth "as it is in Heaven" (Matt. 6:9-14), but we are to live and work in such a way that this prayer comes true in our lives. The most elementary understanding of God should convince even the newest believer that the Creator of everything which exists would not have created man with the ability to develop dreams and goals but without the capacity to make them come true.

Each person is born with the "seed" of greatness. There are very few people who do not have dreams and goals in their hearts as teenagers and young adults. However, millions of people — even Christians — now live mundane existences.

Those "seeds" have never sprouted and grown into fulfillment. The dreams and goals have not matured to bear fruit.

You, dear reader, were born a "king" with an unlimited potential to create your own "empire." The principles you can learn through reading this book will show you how much time and energy you have been wasting by simply "making do," or "making a living." Wishing will never make it so, but beginning to apply these principles in every area of your life right where you are will begin to "make it so."

From this day forward, you can accept your inheritance, possess your empire, create your kingdom, and begin the lifelong process outlined in *The Making of a King*.

> — Jim Stovall, Co-founder and President
> Narrative Television Network
> Tulsa, Oklahoma

Preface

The Making of a King is offered as a book of practical spiritual "psychology" for ambitious Christians, the achievers, whether in business or ministry. It is based upon the story of the call, consecration, and culturization of Saul, the first king of Israel, as shown in 1 Samuel 9,10.

To catch the essence of the principles dealt with in this book and to make the connection with the story of King Saul, I would suggest that 1 Samuel 9-11 be read, preferably from *The Living Bible*, before reading this book.

Those chapters tell the real story of a real person who actually lived. They are not a spiritual allegory or parable. The story of Saul contains the important events of the first king of the nation of Israel. Saul, of the tribe of Benjamin, lived out the events chronicled in the Bible.

His life, as well as the other events of the Old Testament, were written down and preserved for our benefit: for instruction, correction, emulation of the righteous things, avoidance of the unrighteous, and inspiration. (1 Cor. 10:11; 2 Tim. 3:16.)

— Tom Leding
Tulsa, Oklahoma

Introduction

Everything in space obeys the laws of physics. If you know these laws and obey them, space will treat you kindly. . . .[1]

– Dr. Wernher Von Braun

If German scientist Wernher Von Braun's statement quoted above is accurate pertaining to space and its laws, the Creator also has established laws governing the spiritual, psychological, economic, and social areas of life. We are given glimpses of this all through Scripture.

For example, in 2 Chronicles 27:6, the writer recorded this: **Jotham grew powerful because he walked steadfastly before the Lord his God.** *The King James Version* is more succinct: **Jotham became mighty, because he ordered his ways before his God.**

If Jotham, king of Judah and son of the great King Uzziah of the prophet Jeremiah's day, could successfully plan and execute his life in that ancient and primitive time, we can do the same today.

The concepts in this book are based on things gleaned during many years of Bible study, combined with approximately

198 credit hours of college work in various fields, exposure to some of the greatest books on self-improvement ever written by some of the greatest achievers ever known, and years of experience in sales and business.

Of particular importance was the experience gained during the most traumatic years of my business life — the early to mid-80s. Along with the nation, I went through several economic recessions. The stress of working in such times resulted in what could be expected: loss of confidence and physical exhaustion.

Through counseling, I established a new set of goals for my life. I developed a biblical seven-year plan to get myself out of the economic desert created by the "years of famine" I had just been through. To use yet another metaphor: By "pulling myself out of the morass" of problems through the use of the principles in this book, I proved them valid, workable, and efficacious.

Other sources of these principles were some wise sayings by sages of the ages, However, quoting the principles or wise sayings of a certain scientist, author, philosopher, or even minister *does not mean I agree with or endorse everything that person has said or written.*

I have used some of this material in lessons presented and discussed in a businessman's Christian Tip Club breakfast and in years of lectures as a motivational speaker. However, no writer or speaker with something valid to say ever "starts from scratch." As the early Latin philosopher Lucan wrote:

Pygmies placed on the shoulders of giants see more
than the giants themselves.[2]

Other sources of these practical concepts of how to live a successful life are the lives of people I have known or read about who have accomplished great things. Many great achievers seem to have succeeded from the time of their first efforts. However, others bounce back to success only after one, or perhaps repeated, failures.

Knowledge has been gleaned from all these sources, but the greatest inspiration to me has been personal interviews with achievers whenever intrusion into their private lives has been welcomed, or at least, permitted.

The validity of these principles as they have been "worked out" left me with the inspiration to spend untold hours writing this book and enabled me to be bold enough to challenge others to prove them also.

In several brief chapters, I have listed and discussed almost 40 things one must have, do, be, or achieve to become a "king" in one's chosen field. All can be found in, or inferred from, the life story of King Saul.

Not unexpectedly, many of my well-read, Bible-loving friends expressed surprise that I chose Saul's life to use as the basis for such a book, considering the sad turn of events in the tragic years just before his ignoble death. However, I believe his ultimate failure only strengthens, not weakens, my premise:

If high ideals can lead to great achievement, the loss of those ideals would, in turn, lead to great failure, destroying one's life.

One might call Saul's story "The Making *and the Unmaking* of a King." Logan Pearsall Smith observed:

When they come downstairs from their Ivory Towers, Idealists are apt to walk straight into the gutter.[3]

Jesus, in His characteristically salient way of stating important principles, put it this way:

When an evil spirit comes out of a man, it goes through arid places seeking rest, and does not find it ... Then it goes and takes with it seven other spirits

more wicked than itself, and they go in and live there. And the final condition of that man is worse than the first. . . .

Matthew 12:43,45

If anything can be observed clearly about great achievers, it is that strong character traits and strong wills enabled them to succeed. They carry with them from childhood the seeds of greatness and the possibility — if not the probability — of equally great failure; hence the adage, "The higher one climbs, the greater the fall."

One who studies the lives of Bible heroes can see this is true of Jacob, Moses, David, Job, Peter, and others. Also, this can be seen in the lives of great men in all walks of life throughout history. How many men who were great in various fields in their lifetimes now are unknown? There are many such.

It is easily demonstrable that what it takes to "get a good thing going" is also what it takes to "keep a good thing going."

Saul, failing to maintain high ideals, walked straight into the "gutter," so to speak. God always places before us the ability to make a choice to do the right thing. Using common sense and sticking to our principles enables us not only to get going but to keep going.

English author Owen Feltham wrote years ago that:

The greatest results in life are usually attained by simple means and the exercise of ordinary qualities. These may for the most part be summed up in these two — *common sense and perseverance.*[4]

Irish dramatist George Bernard Shaw once said that people always blame "circumstances" for what and who they are.

I might add that people should more accurately blame who they are for their circumstances. Actually, I do not believe in "circumstances" as a factor in one's failure.

I agree with Shaw when he said successful people are:

The people who get up and look for the circumstances they want and, if they can't find them, make them.[5]

Most of us have grown tired of hearing about the success of one who "builds a better mousetrap," but it is still true. This is a person who not only has taken charge of his circumstances, but actually has shaped them.

If a man can write a better book, preach a better sermon, or make a better mouse-trap than his neighbor, though he build his house in the woods, the world will make a beaten path to his door.[6]

As we "dig into" and study the life of Saul, you will discover many of the choices he made in reaction to events, choices that came out of his nature and shaped his character. This is not to say that this book is an exhaustive analysis of his life. However, what we can see will give us guidelines to right choices and decisions, even in a vastly different time and culture.

---

[1]Von Braun, Wernher. *Time Magazine*, Feb. 17, 1958.

[2]Lucan (Marcus A. Lucanus, A.D. 39-65, Iberian-born Roman poet). "Pharsalia," *Lucan's Wisdom*.

[3]Brussell, Eugene E. *Webster's New World Dictionary of Quotable Definitions*, (Englewood Cliffs, NJ: Prentice Hall, 1988, 1970), "Idealist," p. 273.

[4]*The New Dictionary of Thoughts*, (Standard Book Company, 1965), "Success," p. 645.

[5]*Dictionary of Quotable Definitions*, "Success," p. 549.

[6]*New Dictionary of Thoughts*, p. 645.

1

Get Your Values Straight

Ninety percent of failures are due to the lack of a clear, definite goal.

Saul was the son of a Benjamite named Kish, whom the Bible calls "a mighty man of power" and "a choice young man" (1 Sam. 9:1 KJV.) The NIV says he was "an impressive young man without equal among the Israelites," standing head and shoulders taller than anyone else. (1 Sam. 9:2.)

Not only was Saul in good physical shape, but he came of good heritage. He should have had his values straight from childhood. In fact, the very first incident we are told about in his life shows setting priorities, determining goals, and making decisions as to what was important; in other words, *setting values*, the first step toward achievement.

Saul is introduced to us when his father sent him with a servant to search for some lost donkeys. After three days of looking throughout his tribe's territory, Saul and the servant had used up all of their food and almost all of their money. Obviously discouraged, Saul's decision about what was important was this:

> ... Come, let's go back, or my father will stop thinking about the donkeys and start worrying about us.

> **1 Samuel 9:5**

He had left home with the priority of finding the lost animals and the goal of searching neighboring territory until he found them. Now, after three days of fruitless searching, he had sense enough to see that things had changed. Now his priority was to get home before his father sent a search party out after him! Great achievers have the ability to change when necessary.

Unless your values are straight, you will live aimlessly without a specific goal in mind. An old tenant farmer once said to his son, "You aint' going nowhar 'til you start for somewhar." A well-known adage puts it this way: For a ship bound for no harbor, no wind can be favorable.

In other words, before you can get anywhere, you must decide where you want to go.

The Power of a Definite Goal or Purpose

In this chapter, I want to answer these questions: Does the Bible really mean that, "as a man thinketh in his heart, so is he"? (Prov. 23:7.) Does that verse mean that we can *think* our way to success? Does goal setting really work? If so, why? What makes it work?

I have found personally — and in studying the lives of others — that goal setting *does* work. One reason is that, if one has an aim, goal, destination, aspiration, or dream to which his heart is "welded" and unconditionally committed, he will make things happen to achieve this. A motivational talk I often present is entitled "Success and Prosperity Is a Planned Event."

To begin where Saul did, evaluate your life and see what you want to accomplish. What do you want to gain? It will help to write down your major goals or purposes. Set your goal, your destination. Make a plan. Picture the achieving of it in your mind so that it is a fixed goal, not simply a wish or a hope.

In my experience, a very good way to get one's values straight and to operate within God's principles is to study the book of Proverbs written by King Solomon. By studying one chapter a day, you will get through the book in a month.

Solomon, the third king of Israel, was respected in his time as wiser than all surrounding rulers. (1 Kings 4:30,31.) In fact, God said there had been no one like him before and would be no one like him afterwards. (1 Kings 3:12.)

As you read his words, you will find wisdom that covers all areas of life. From winning and keeping friends to losing bets, from giving counsel to accepting correction, Proverbs predicts happiness or disaster as this advice is followed. All of these comments and principles came from Solomon's experience of testing and proving God's wisdom in life situations. He advises us how man can relate harmoniously to his fellowman, as long as he maintains a right relationship with God.

The author of 3,000 proverbs (wise sayings and principles of life) and 1,000 songs possessed extraordinary credentials for describing the wise, successful life. Early in his career, he prayed:

"So give your servant a discerning heart to govern your people and to distinguish between right and wrong. For who is able to govern this great people of yours?"

1 Kings 3:9

Because Solomon asked for wisdom and understanding instead of great wealth and a long life, he received all of those things from God. (1 Kings 3:11,12.) He began like Saul by getting his values straight and setting priorities toward his goal in life: to "judge" (govern) God's people as God willed.

As you read the book, you will find again and again that it could have been written specifically to you. Proverbs includes

3

advice about gaining money (22:1), establishing peace (16:7), fortifying integrity (21:2), strengthening marriages (31:30), building a business (24:34), avoiding seducers (6:32), resisting bribes (15:27), overcoming strife (15:1), and countless other experiences that plague or exalt everyday life.

Wisdom comes alive in these writings and promises that:

For whoever finds me finds life and receives favor from the Lord. But whoever fails to find me harms himself; all who hate me love death.

Proverbs 8:35,36

The book of Proverbs is the answer to what is wrong with the world; *the reader is the answer to what can be done about it.*

Proverbs 14:26 and 32 sum up the achievements of a good life:

He who fears the Lord has a secure fortress, and for his children it will be a refuge .... When calamity comes, the wicked are brought down, but even in death the righteous have a refuge.

I have used the precepts from Proverbs in my own life to help build confidence in my ability to be successful. Let's sum up what you can do in order to set the right values for your own life.

Ten Guidelines for Setting Values

1. Get a vision and stamp it indelibly on your mind as a mental picture of yourself succeeding. Hold this picture tenaciously. Never permit it to fade. Your mind is the "darkroom worker" that will seek to "develop" this picture. Always "picture" success, no matter how badly things may be going at the moment.

2. Never doubt the reality of the mental image, and never think of yourself as failing. If you truly believe, you will

4

receive whatever you ask for in prayer. (Matt. 21:22.) Do not build up obstacles in your imagination. Depreciate and minimize every possible obstacle.

3. For every negative thought that comes to mind, deliberately cancel it out with a positive one.

4. Difficulties must be studied and efficiently dealt with. However, to be eliminated, they must be seen objectively, not inflated by imagination or fear.

5. Do not be awestruck by other people so that you try to mimic them. No one can be *you* as efficiently as you can. Most people, in spite of confident demeanor and appearance, often are more doubtful of their abilities than you are of yours and, perhaps, as frightened.

6. Try to understand why you do what you do. Learn the origin of your inferiority and self-doubt. This often begins in childhood.

Recently, one of the most obnoxious and weird radio talk show hosts was asked why he is the way he is. His reply was that his father always called him a moron, so he guessed he learned to act like one. The man was laughing, apparently thinking that was a funny remark, but it was the absolute bottom line on why his personality developed the way it did.

He has "ridden" that source of inferiority to achieve his goals, but in a very negative way. A Christian with such a handicap can go to his real Father, God, and replace the negative with positive characteristics and thinking. Self-knowledge can, and ought to, lead to a cure for what ails you.

7. If you have any fear or negative programming in your mind, practice the following affirmation by repeating it out loud at least five times a day: **I can do all things through Christ which strengtheneth**

me (Phil. 4:13 KJV). That promise written by the Apostle Paul is the most powerful antidote on earth to inferiority thoughts.

8. Make as true an estimate as you can of your own abilities, then raise it 20 percent. Do not become egotistical, thinking "more highly" of yourself than you ought (Rom. 12:3), but develop a wholesome self-respect.

9. Believe in your own God-released powers that come from submitting to God's will and putting yourself in His hands. Pray simply, "God, I am now by an act of my will placing myself totally in Your hands." Then believe you are receiving through the Holy Spirit adequate power to meet life's demands, to overcome the world and the enemy. (Luke 10:19.) "Feel" it flowing into you, Jesus said "the Kingdom of God is within you" (Luke 17:2).

10. Five times a day, repeat this dynamic truth: **If God be for us, who can be against us?** (Rom. 8:31). Stop reading now and repeat these words slowly and confidently. Do they not already made a difference in your confidence level? Remind yourself often that God is with you, therefore you cannot be defeated, no matter how circumstances look. There is a way to be victorious.

True success is founded on character.

Personality is what you show to others; character is what you are.

Without "the right stuff" (character), these guidelines will be just so many words, not real values.

2

Develop Character, Not Ego

Character is like a tree and reputation like its shadow.
(Abraham Lincoln) Character is that which reveals moral
purpose, exposing the class of things a man chooses or
avoids. (Aristotle)[1]

Saul gained a kingdom, but could not retain the throne. The reason is very conspicuous in his story, more by its absence than by its presence. The reason is *character*. Saul did not have it by nature, nor did he develop it by culture. Instead, he developed a "healthy" ego, which was very "unhealthy" for him.

The right values of the Israelites instilled in him at home apparently were only "skin deep," even at the age of 30 when he became king. (1 Sam. 13:1 TLB.) He learned values mentally, and apparently operated on "programmed" behavior until he gained authority over the nation. Then the lack of real character was revealed.

Saul never developed a heart that followed after God's heart in obedience, as did his successor, David. (Acts 13:22.) Character comes out of the heart, not the mind. It is very easy to think one thing and do another without a strong character.

Millions of Americans have heard the gifted and powerful motivational speaker, Cavitt Roberts, and to him I am indebted

7

for one of the best definition of character I have ever heard. Roberts credits this definition to one of his professors. Paraphrased, it is this:

> Real character is the ability to push through to a final
> conclusion a determination made during a moment
> of high emotion and dedication, long after the mood
> is gone.

One might say that many marriages fail today because of a lack of real character, a lack of determination to carry through with something after the moment of high emotion is gone. The same is true of making a success of one's career, of ministry, of parenting, and of business. What carries us through the hard times, the down times, the times when nothing goes right, is *character*.

There is little scope for character to show up in leadership during good times. Any "king" or "queen" looks good during coronation ceremonies. Character shows in times of trouble and confusion. We can see this in the British royal family during the troubles of the pre-World War II decade.

King Edward VIII, better known as the Duke of Windsor, abdicated his responsibilities to his people to follow his own desires. On the other hand, his brother, whom we know as King George VI, stood like a rock in spite of great timidity and ill health. Both men were born of the same parents and reared in the same culture, yet one had character and one did not.

Saul and David were not natural or even tribal brothers, yet both were born Israelites and reared in the same culture. Saul never developed real character, and David seems always to have had it. Of course, for a child of God today, character is founded on a relationship with the Father and a determination to model oneself on Jesus, beginning with attitudes of the heart. (Matt. 15:18.)

In contrast to Saul, several kings of Judah showed great character, but few kings of Israel. For example, King Asa, the great-great-grandson of David, displayed the ingredients of character that provided leadership for the people. We find this in 2 Chronicles 15:14,15 TLB:

> **They shouted out their oath of loyalty to God with trumpets blaring and horns sounding. All were happy for this covenant with God, for they had entered into it with *all their hearts and wills*, and wanted him above everything else, and they found him! And he gave them peace throughout the nation.**

Asa not only removed idols from the land but removed his own mother from her position as "Queen Mother," because she had made an idol. Because of Asa's character, the people in the nation of Judah had 25 more years without war.

It took courage for Asa to do what he did, which in his day ran counter to the culture and desires of the people. Judah had become permeated with idolatry. Many prophets even told them down through the years that they loved their idols more than their God. Asa could have been assassinated, but he had the courage to do the right thing even if it meant taking a risk.

Courage is a foundation stone of character.

Courage: a Foundation Stone

Perhaps the bottom line about character was said by the Latin writer, Publilius Syrus, which is that character is the arbiter (the determiner) of a man's fortune. Other quotes from well-known people that may help us understand character are these:

- Raising your soul so high that offence cannot reach it.

  (Adapted from Rene Descartes)

- A development which is higher than intellect.

  (Norman Elright)

9

- Mastery over your thoughts and actions. (Gandhi)

- (That which) must stand behind and back up everything — the sermon, the poem, the picture, the play. None of them is worth a straw without it. (Josiah G. Holland)

- The measure of a man's character is what he would do if he knew he would never be found out. (T. B. Macauley) Or, according to the great 19th-century preacher Dwight L. Moody, "(Character is) what you are in the dark."[2]

In the first event in Saul's story, we can see the seeds of success, which, if cultivated, would have caused character to develop. We can see as well the seeds of negativity that eventually led to the failure of Saul's kingship and life. If those seeds had been overcome, his story would have ended differently.

The negative seeds were fear of poverty and fear of man (fear of rejection or of what others might think). At the very end of his life, he cared more about what the people thought of him than what God and the prophet thought. (1 Sam. 15:30.)

Then Saul pleaded again, "I have sinned; but oh, at least honor me before my people. . . ."

So we can see that one of the facets of character is courage to do the right thing in spite of the consequences or what other people may think. To get *courage* firmed up in one's heart, fear must be overcome.

Courage is not the lack of fear, but overcoming fear to do what needs to be done.

---

[1]*Dictionary of Quotable Definitions*, "Character," p. 73.
[2]Ibid.

3
Overcoming Fear

No great idea, project, or achievement is without challenges and risks that can "scare us half to death."

When Saul came to the realization that his goal (finding the donkeys) was not going to be achieved by the procedures he was using and in the time he felt was feasible, he changed goals: Go home before his father began to worry and send a search party after them. However, the servant had a better idea. That was to visit the prophet of God and ask for spiritual guidance in finding the donkeys.

Saul's fear of poverty and fear of rejection surfaced at this point, as we can see in his question, "But, what do we have to give him so that he will help us? We have eaten up all the food we brought." (1 Sam. 9:7.)

He was afraid the prophet would not receive them without an honorarium, according to the custom. Not much later at his "coronation ceremony," he hid because of his fear of failure in carrying out his responsibilities. (1 Sam. 10:20-22.)

Ralph Waldo Emerson wrote, "The wise man in the storm prays to God, not for safety from danger but for deliverance from fear."[1]

11

Sixteenth-century French essayist-philosopher Montaigne expressed it this way: "He who fears he shall suffer already suffers what he fears."[2] To defeat fear, use the power of bigger dreams. Many people achieve little in life because they are afraid to dream big dreams. They aim too low. Successful men and women are great dreamers.

Think of a big, grand dream to work toward, a dream that can bring great joy when you achieve it. Remember: big dreams, big achievements; small dreams, small achievements. If your dream is practical, reach for it; or, as the world says, "Go for it!"

What would you attempt to do if you knew you could not fail?

Plato, perhaps the most famous of the Greek philosophers, taught his students to take charge of their thoughts. Someone else has written that we should guard our thoughts well, because they are "heard in heaven."[3]

All of us have far greater powers to overcome fears, conquer weaknesses, and master conflicts than we have yet demonstrated and far more ability to live greater lives. No one ever learns to live until he has awakened the dormant power within him.

One day, I sat on the steps of a church and prayed the most desperate prayer of my entire life:

"Please help me, God. Please change me. I know You can, because I have seen You make drunkards sober and turn thieves into honest men. Please take away these inferiority feelings that are holding me back. Take away this awful shyness and self-consciousness. Let me see myself, not as a scared rabbit, but as someone who can do great things in life because You are with me, giving me the strength and confidence I need."

As the years went by, I began using the Bible promises as literally to and for me, verses such as 2 Timothy 1:7:

For God did not give us a spirit of timidity, but a spirit of power, of love and of self-discipline.

I soon realized that my thinking must be fueled by God's grace through prayer, faith, obedience, and diligence. I was fortunate enough to discover an image of success that was stronger than my original image of failure.

This image is very simple: *If you think you can, or someone who believes in you thinks you can — why, you can!*

You must visualize the image of yourself succeeding so vividly that, when the desired success comes, it seems to be merely echoing a reality that already exists. A person who is not single-minded is certain to fail. You must be committed to your goals and dreams.

In fact, scientific experiments have shown that merely acting positive helps produce positive emotions and outlooks that help you succeed.

There *Is* Power in Thinking Positively

In recent years, perhaps there has been too much emphasis on "positive thinking," because too many have taught it or tried to use it as "cure-all" for everything from lack of character to outright failure. Although positive thinking will not cover shortcomings, the truth remains that there *is* power in thinking positively.

A salesperson must feel good about himself or herself in order to be effective. You must believe in yourself and in your product or service.

An entrepreneur must see opportunities and go after them, which is not possible if he is "down" on himself.

The difference between committed people and those who only have a passing interest in achieving a goal is that committed people keep their agreements with themselves.

Those with a wish or a hope, a passing interest in a certain goal, always have some reason for *not* achieving it, such as, "Perhaps the time is not quite right," or "The plan must have been wrong to begin with." (If the plan truly was wrong, I will deal in a later chapter with backing up to where you missed it.)

For people who have made a choice and have the commitment to achieve, there are no such mumbled excuses. Goals are not finessed, negotiated, or glimpsed from a distance. They are pursued fiercely and single-mindedly.

Some people flounder around in hazy situations, but true entrepreneurs prosper by taking advantage of innovative projects on their own.

Of course, you will see mistakes on a regular basis. Walking toward a set goal does not always proceed along a smooth path. In fact, I get nervous if I do not see a few hindrances or obstacles. Success and growth occur only when you proceed along a new path, or do new things, or do old things a new way.

Zeno the Stoic, a Cyprian-born Greek philosopher who lived three centuries before Jesus, already knew more about fear than many of us. He said that *fear is the expectation of evil.*[4]

In a sense, fear is negative faith, believing in bad things happening rather than good. Zeno wrote also:

Under fear are arranged the following emotions: terror, nervous shrinking, shame, consternation, panic, mental agony. *Terror* is fear which produces fright; *shame* is fear of disgrace; *nervous shrinking* is a fear that one will have to act; *consternation* is fear due to a presentation of some unusual occurrence; *panic* is fear with pressure exercised by sound; *mental agony* is fear felt when some issue is still in suspense.[5]

Dream a dream, *then stick with it!* Give your fears over to the Lord as sin, as doubt in His ability to keep you. We need to follow the pattern of our Lord Jesus Christ, who did all things well and was consumed with zeal for God. Zeal for doing God's will cannot help but give you a positive outlook on yourself and on life.

[1]Emerson, Ralph Waldo.

[2]Seldes, George. *The Great Thoughts*, (New York: Ballantine Books, a division of Random House, Inc.; copyright 1985 by Seldes, new compilation by David Laskin, 1996), p. 329; Montaigne, Michel Eyquem de (1533-1592), *Essays*, Bk. III, Ch. 13.

[3]*New Dictionary of Thoughts*, "Thoughts," p. 669.

[4]*The Great Thoughts*, p. 512; Zeno the Stoic (335-263 B.C.).

[5]Ibid.

4

Assess Your Situation

To escape from a dilemma, there is no substitute for knowing who you are, what you are, where you are, and the general status of what is.

The American Cancer Society says thousands of lives per year could be saved *if people were not afraid to be examined.* One of the pioneers in modern psychiatry is said to have studied the lives of outstanding people and found one of their most important characteristics has been a superior (above average) perception of reality.

Self-actualizers have the ability to see life as it is rather than as they wish it to be. The ability to be realistic, particularly when it concerns an unpleasant truth about oneself, is a vital part of good emotional health. People who can see reality — but at the same time have a valid vision or dream of how reality can be changed — make better judgments, are more creative, and are quicker to cooperate with others wanting to change.

Steven Spiegel, author of a book on America's Middle East policy since World War II, points out how most changes occur:

Spiegel challenges the belief that American policy in the Middle East primarily reacts to events in that

17

region. On the contrary, he finds that . . . it is the next administration (after the one in which the events occurred) that produces new ideas in response to the last crisis.[1]

Companies do this as well as individuals. It is human nature, somehow, to react to crises rather than heading them off. One who sees reality will see a crisis shaping up and adjust his actions accordingly, not wait until something happens and then change to fit that situation.

It is good to learn from one's mistakes. However, what if that situation never occurs again and you have changed your policy or operations to cope with it? Then you are once again in the wrong place doing the wrong thing when something different happens. This sort of policy making is rather like closing the barn door after the horse is gone.

Hindsight is said to be better than foresight, but that is true only if you do not have real foresight.

When Saul decided to give up and go home, he was right to be concerned about his father's feelings. However, he was not seeing reality in the sense that there was something else that could be done before giving up. The servant assessed the situation more accurately.

In essence, he said, "I've just realized something. We are near the town where the great prophet Samuel lives. I've heard that everything he says comes true. Perhaps he can tell us where the donkeys are so that we will not have to return emptyhanded." (1 Sam. 9:6.)

However, Saul was afraid the prophet would not receive them, because they had nothing to give him, having eaten up all their food. At that point, he did not know where he was, who or what he was (a king in the making), or the reality of the situation. Also, he did not "recognize" reality when he heard it:

They were near a prophet's home, the man probably could tell them what they wanted to know, and the servant had a piece of silver so they would not have to approach Samuel emptyhanded.

Through Jeremiah, a much later prophet, God gave the Israelites in the nation of Judah good advice for assessing one's situation:

Once again, give them this message from the Lord: When a person falls, he jumps up again; when he is on the wrong road and discovers his mistake, he goes back to the fork where he made the wrong turn. But these people keep on along their evil path, though I warn them.

Jeremiah 8:4,5 TLB

How Far Do You Want To Go?

Whatever failures I have known, whatever errors I have committed have been the consequences of action without thought, action without truly assessing my situation. The potential for reaching goals depends on how far you want to go. If you find yourself on "the wrong road," do you have the courage to go back to the "fork"?

Thomas Edison said success is based on imagination plus ambition and the will to work. Have the courage to face the truth about your situation. Success follows proper motivation. Without a vision, the people perish, God said (Hos. 4:6), and without direction, you might as well "go home without the donkeys."

It is important to keep your promises to others. Keeping one's word is extremely important to God. It is just as important to keep your promises to yourself. The best thing is not to make a promise *unless you intend to do everything possible to fulfill it*. This is the reality that Saul's servant saw.

At the beginning of any undertaking, whether it seems easy or doubtful, believing you can succeed ensures the successful outcome of your goal. (Mark 9:23.) The basic factor in success is to believe in what you are doing or have set yourself to do.

It is vital to understand that people no smarter, no richer, and no more educated than you have succeeded, even in spite of physical handicaps. One of the founders of a large greeting card firm built a multi-million dollar business from his wheelchair.

Lives of great and successful men prove that even the dull, the poor, the nobodies, the little-schooled, can gain fame and fortune. One thing all successful people have in common is this: They believe in themselves.

Believe that you will succeed, and more than likely, you will. What do you believe about yourself? When you expect the best, it releases a magnetic force in your mind that tends to bring the best to you. This is called "the law of attraction." Like is drawn to like.

However, if you expect the worst, that is what you will get. The ancient wealthy citizen, Job, is a classic example. He said that what he "feared" had come upon him. (Job 3:25.) Faith is simply belief — faith in God and His Word, faith in yourself, and faith in the Holy Spirit's guidance in life.

Jesus said that, if you have faith, nothing will be impossible. (Matt. 9:29.) Assess your situation, go back to the place you made the wrong turn if possible, and then *believe* that, with God's help, you can and will reach your goal. Instill in your mind and heart the truth that *faith moves mountains*.

How do you assess a situation? The 19th century British writer Rudyard Kipling summed up the procedure for assessing any situation in words that for years were the guidelines of newspaper reporters and editors:

I keep six honest serving men;

(They taught me all I knew)

Their names are *What* and *Where* and *When*

And *How* and *Why* and *Who*.[2]

Use those six "serving men" to analyze whatever situation you are in. The answers to those six questions will reveal the truth to you. Then utilize the same short questions to assess where you want to go — and believe that, by taking the right road, you will reach the planned destination.

---

[1]Spiegel, Steven L. *The Other Arab-Israeli Conflict*, (Chicago: The University of Chicago Press, 1985), From front cover endnotes.

[2]Beecroft, John, Ed. *Kipling: A Selection of His Stories and Poems*, Vol. I, (Garden City, N.Y.: Doubleday & Company, Inc., 1956), Just So Stories, "The Elephant's Child," p. 383.

5
Be Willing To Ask For
and Receive Help

If you are reluctant to ask the way, you will be lost.

— Malay Proverb

Dr. Robert Schuller, founder and pastor of Crystal Cathedral near Los Angeles, is also a great applied psychologist. He says that, for millions of people, the three hardest words to say are, "I need help."

Most of us men can identify with this reluctance in such a simple thing as stopping to ask for directions. Our wives are saying to stop here or there or ask this one or that one, but we are reluctant to do so because of pride. Yet, sometimes, we have to admit we do not know where we are or how to get to where we want to go. The alternative is to waste time, energy, and money muddling around in a maze.

In life, some people remain lost forever for lack of enough humility to ask for help in finding one's way.

No one who ever became a great success got there on his (or her) own. It is as important to be a gracious receiver as a gracious giver in any area of life. It takes humility to be either. The "meek" (the humble in spirit, or those willing to be taught) are those who will inherit the earth, Jesus said. (Matt. 5:5.)

The late Vance Havner, one of America's best-loved and most quoted preachers, said:

> When I started out preaching, it made me nervous when a "big preacher" showed up in the congregation. I have learned since that a really big preacher is the easiest of all men to preach to. If he just *thinks* he is a big preacher, he *needs* preaching to![1]

A person who only "thinks" he or she is a "big" anything will not receive help, much less ask for it. That person, whether he realizes it or not, has begun to "die on the vine." Such a person is like a plant that stands tall in the sun but refuses to put forth its roots underground toward water. Before long, it will wither and die.

In the beginning of his "career," Saul was willing to receive help. He immediately accepted the servant's offer of silver for Samuel and said, "Okay, let's go to the seer!" (1 Sam. 9:10.) On the way, they met some girls and were not too proud to ask directions to find Samuel.

By being willing to ask for and receive help, Saul found the prophet, then found that Samuel knew all about him as well as where the donkeys could be found — even before he asked. Samuel told him the animals already had been found.

However, unfortunately for Saul and for Israel, he did not remain in an attitude of humility. Instead, as Saul achieved more and more success in his kingly role, he became proud, and no longer would he ask for or receive help. Success must not be allowed to "go to the head," which causes problems in the heart.

A truly successful person, a truly great person, has humility.

A truly successful person does not mind asking other people to help him — if or when he needs help to achieve his goals.

A truly successful person knows he can hire other people to do what he cannot — or what he does not know how to do — to complete his dream or to bring his idea to completion. If you lack money, knowledge, or skill, you can get others who have these things to work for you providing you have a good idea and great confidence in that idea.

Scottish-born Andrew Carnegie, the richest man in the world in 1901, only had about four years of schooling and did not know much about steel. His first investment in railroad-related stock was made with $50 from a mortgage his mother took on their home in Pennsylvania. Yet he became the "steel king" of America, leaving almost $23 million at his death in 1918, a great fortune for that time.

When I read biographies of great men and observe the lives of those living today, I find that each of them knew what he wanted and exercised great patience and perseverance in getting to his goal.

I know one man who is a billionaire at 40 years of age and is headed toward becoming the richest man in the world today. He knows what he wants and is pursuing it diligently and patiently.

Wealth Is Not Always Success

There are many in our society who look successful because of their position and/or wealth. However, if you examine their lives, you will see that they are not really prospering.

John D. Rockefeller Jr., one of America's all-time richest and most successful men, said, "The poorest man I know is the man who has nothing but money."[2] Even Carnegie wrote in his early career that amassing wealth is one of the worst species of idolatry.[3]

Money does not make success, although God does not want His people to live in poverty. Poverty is a curse. God intended His people to be the "head" and not the "tail." (Deut. 28:13.) However, in the pattern of Old Testament Israel, we can see that blessings in all areas of life *follow*, not precede, obedience to Him. (Deut. 28:1-14.)

Fulfilling God's plan for your life and prospering in all areas of spirit, soul, and body, makes one a success. I guarantee that you will not achieve such prosperity without taking some risks. However, let's digress from risk-taking a moment and discuss money, riches, and wealth.

The Babylonian Empire was the most prosperous kingdom in ancient history, because its people appreciated the value of wealth. They practiced sound financial principles in acquiring wealth, keeping wealth, and making that wealth earn more. They provided for themselves what we all desire: wealth for the future.

Most of us go through life hoping God will bestow riches upon us, without going to His Word and finding out the criteria necessary to receive blessings. Deuteronomy 8:18 says it is God who gives the power to get wealth. Even Babylon was blessed in its early years, in spite of paganism and barbarity, because God had His hand on that empire as a place where His people could prosper in exile. (Jer. 27:5-11, 29:28.)

Is God not good? The Israelites in the southern nation of Judah finally had sinned to such iniquity that the final curse of Deuteronomy 28 came upon them: eviction and permanent exile from their land. In spite of their wickedness and hardness of heart, as delineated in Isaiah, Jeremiah, and Ezekiel, God's mercy went ahead of them to provide a place for them to live in happiness and contentment and set a time limit on the exile. (Jer. 25:12.)

Babylon's downfall came when they began to *worship* money. Paul wrote that the root of *all* evil is the *love* of money, not money itself. (1 Tim. 6:10.) King Nebuchadnezzar sounded the deathknell of the country when he had a huge gold bar constructed as an idol for everyone to bow down and worship. (Dan. 3:1-6.)

The story of how three Hebrew youths withstood the command to worship this image of wealth is told in Daniel 3:8-30. In Christian society today, we have two extremes of thinking about money, both of which are wrong:

1. Money itself is evil, and poverty is next to godliness.

2. Wealth is from God, therefore, if a Christian is poor, he lacks faith or is into some kind of sin.

Actually, we have seen some of the wealthiest ministries fall in the past decade because the focus was on prosperity, not God.

The Apostle Paul called those who judged a person's spirituality by his wealth "men of corrupt minds, and destitute of the truth." (1 Tim. 6:5.) He told the early Christians to separate themselves from those who supposed "gain was godliness." However, Paul was talking still about the *love* of money. He never said money itself was evil or having it was wrong.

The sinfulness comes in your attitude toward money or your motivation for getting it. There are many reasons why Christians are poor, none of them being God's doing. Perhaps it *is* lack of faith; however, more often, the reason for poverty can be found in the mind, the way one thinks about prosperity and about oneself.

One purpose of writing this book is to bring to readers an understanding of why poverty is in their lives — if it is — and how they can move from poverty to the blessings of God. In Deuteronomy 28 and Leviticus 26, God made it perfectly plain that He does not see poverty as a blessing.

There are more scriptures in the Bible on prosperity than any other topic. The road to wealth is yours, when you learn that God is your provider, your Father, and that Jesus is your "boss." Therefore all you have is God's. Yet he allows you to keep 90 percent for your own use. Keeping His portion, however, makes you a thief with no right to blessings. (Mal. 3:30,11.)

Wealth like a tree grows from a tiny seed. The sooner you begin to give God His 10 percent, then put at least 10 percent in savings or investments, the quicker your "money tree" will grow. If you spend all you make, the will to succeed is not in you.

I have found it is hard to get people to start with a "seed," in other words to start small. Begin with $5, if that is all you have. Most people think they have to start with hundreds instead of ones. A lean bank account is easier to cure than to endure.

Learn to make money work for you. The only way to do this is to sit down and make out a workable budget, taking a little from wherever possible to put in savings. Then begin to look for ways to make extra money.

Men of action are the ones who get ahead. However, be careful where you invest your money. Seek sound business counsel from those who are expert in these things (ask for help, in other words), but do not neglect praying for a witness from God. If you have an inward peace about an investment, do it. Better a little caution than a great regret, but do not be afraid to take a risk.

Saul ended up with money, fame, and position, but he did not end up a success. The small seed of pride that we see in his beginning developed into a big tree of stubbornness. The fruit of that tree was rebellion against God.

In his latter days, Samuel said something to Saul quite different than the words he spoke at their first meeting:

> **And Samuel told him, "When you didn't think much of yourself, God made you king of Israel.... Why did you rush for the loot and do exactly what God said not to? ... For rebellion is as bad as the sin of witchcraft, and stubbornness is as bad as worshiping idols."**
>
> **1 Samuel 15:17,19,21** TLB

An epigram gives us a picture of one who has set himself to refuse to ask or receive help from others because of pride or stubbornness: *Some minds are like finished concrete — thoroughly mixed and permanently set.*[4] Such a mind cannot achieve success.

Always treat others as you would be treated, "the Golden Rule." (Matt. 7:12.) Make others feel good about themselves. If you are sincere in your comments made for the good of others, it will come back to you like "bread on the water." (Eccl. 11:1.)

Last but not least, be willing to take risks to win. Hiding behind the baggage train, as Saul did at his coronation, is no way to win anything. Unfortunately, no one usually will drag you out into the limelight.

---

[1]Hester, Dennis J. *The Vance Havner Notebook*, (Grand Rapids: Baker Book House, 1989), p. 256; from Havner's book, *Pepper 'n Salt*, reprinted by Baker, 1983, p. 76.

[2]Tan, Paul Lee. *Encyclopedia of 7700 Illustrations*, (Rockville, MD: Assurance Publishers, 1988), p. 830, #3561.

[3]*A Sense of History, The Best Writing From the Pages of American Heritage*, (New York: American Heritage Press, 1985), p. 431; "Carnegie & Rockefeller, by Robert L. Heilbroner.

[4]*Encyclopedia of 7700 Illustrations*, p. 1362, #6080.

6
Be Willing To Take a Risk

Unless you enter a tiger's den, you cannot take the cubs.
— Japanese Proverb

Nothing is without risk. Living itself is a risk. Taking a short trip to the neighborhood convenience store is a risk. The bigger the stakes, the greater the risks.

Saul never seemed to want to take a risk, but had to be pushed into his position by others: the servant, Samuel, even in the end, the soldiers in his army. He was never a warrior like David, nor a true leader. He tried to eliminate risks from his life, including attempting to assassinate David to stop the risk of losing the throne.

Although the Macbeths were speaking of committing a crime, Shakespeare's words in Lady Macbeth's mouth are true. When her husband said: "If we should fail —," she exclaimed: "(Then) We fail! But screw your courage" (there is that word again) "to the sticking place, and we'll *not* fail."[1] The illimitable "Bard" was a very wise man, almost Solomonic in thinking.

English writer Logan Pearsall Smith also commented on the need for courage to take a risk in life:

31

What is more mortifying than to feel you have missed the plum for *lack of courage* to shake the tree."[2]

The way to have courage to take any risk necessary is to *concentrate on your dream (goal) until you reach it*. If you find yourself still afraid to take a risk, think about the words of a 17th-century French cardinal, "That which is necessary is never a risk."[3] Therefore, the "risks" you take that are necessitated in achieving your goal are not risks at all but proper steps to victory.

Famous British author and Christian apologist G. K. Chesterton had an interesting insight on risk:

I do not believe in a fate that falls on men however they act; but I do believe in a fate that falls on them *unless* they act.[4]

A recent study which I read concluded that successful people tend to brush off failure quickly. They have realized that taking risks that occasionally end in failure is a necessary part of winning a victory.

What unnecessary or low-priority things are distracting you from achieving your goal?

Social scientists and psychologists tell us that more than 90 percent of the information put into our minds each day is of a negative nature. Make a quality decision to sort out and discard the negative. Leave the impossible up to God and get busy with the possible!

A wise man has defined the way getting a vision of our goals and purposes can become real to us:

Vision looks inward and becomes a duty.

Vision looks outward and becomes aspiration.

Vision looks upward and becomes faith.[5]

Define your vision of God's purpose for you and the goal you wish to reach, then let it become necessary (a reality), an aspiration (hope), and finally, absolute belief that with God's help you can achieve it (faith).

Ways To Make Your Vision Real

Security is a state of living that most people seek, yet it can hinder you from reaching your goal. No person ever truly became great by choosing security over the risks necessary to reach a higher goal.

A 17th century English clergyman wrote:

Security is the mother of danger and the grandmother of destruction.[6]

Why would he write that? As a wise Christian leader, Thomas Fuller knew no one ever goes anywhere with "security" as a guide. There is no security outside of Christ. Jobs come and go, economies rise and fall, natural disasters wipe out homes and establishments in the twinkling of an eye, as we have seen in this decade alone.

Be willing to become one whose security is in God, one who is able to take risks to accomplish greater things in this world.

Here are ten ways to cause your vision to become real to you:

1. Decide to change, to become a successful person.

2. Get help by associating with successful people.

3. Get settled in your mind what you want, and stop thinking about what you do not want.

4. Look for the good in people, in what you hear, and in what you see. Keep the negative out of your mind. For example, if your immediate vision is for physical health, stop watching commercials for medicines and so forth. They feed your mind with negative information.

5. See yourself as already having achieved your goal. Use your imagination.

6. Take stock of your skills, things that will help you achieve your goal. Improve them, even by taking night courses, if necessary, or by hours of practicing. Increase your knowledge by studying. It costs nothing to borrow books from a library.

7. Success is rooted in continued effort, so keep trying. Even a turtle must stick its neck out to get somewhere.

8. Have faith in yourself. Without a humble, but reasonable, confidence, you cannot be happy or successful. Self-confidence is an essential ingredient of success.

9. Stand up to any difficulties and refuse to be defeated. Remember: A big "shot" is simply a little "shot" who kept on shooting. When you stand up to difficulties, you get victories. When you get victories, your life will be tremendously enhanced.

10. Last but not least, put your confidence in God. Study His Word for truth and wisdom about prosperity and riches.

By working to "hone" the sharpness of your vision, you will develop a new sense of confidence. Proper preparation is the key to success, and remember your thinking can be no wiser than your understanding. God who began a good work in you will complete it — if you let Him. (Philip. 1:6.)

---

[1]Shakespeare, "Macbeth," *The Oxford Dictionary of Quotations*, (Oxford, England: Oxford University Press, 1941, 1980), p. 459, #10.

[2]Smith, Logan Pearsall.

[3]Seldes. *The Great Thoughts*, p. 385; quote from the *Memoirs of Paul de Gondi, Cardinal de Retz*, Book II.

[4]Chesterton, G.K.

[5]*Dictionary of Quotable Definitions*, p. 592, quote by Stephen S. Wise, under the category of "Vision."

[6]*Great Thoughts*, p. 170; Thomas Fuller (1608-1661, "The Good Judge," Ch. V.

7
Declare Yourself: Make Yourself Known

Our risen Lord cares about each of us personally. I invite you to look at the details in (the letters to the churches, Rev. 3-5). God named names. He described events. . . . He gave them warm, loving, confronting counsel. That alone gives me a tremendous sense of hope. He knows us as a mother knows her child.[1]

– Billy Graham

Who are you? You must know that before you can declare yourself, before you can make your position known. If you are a Christian, then you are these things:

- A child of God, the Creator of the universe who owns all things

- A joint-heir with Jesus, the Son of God, who shed His blood that you might be made a member of a new race, a new creature (2 Cor. 5:17; Gal. 6:15)

- A descendant of Abraham by faith and an inheritor of all the blessings promised to His Seed, Jesus (Gal. 3:29)

- A new creature with the righteousness of Jesus imputed (credited) to him, or her (2 Cor. 5:21)
- A human being, made in the image of God (Gen. 1:26) and reconciled to God (Eph. 2:16), whose eternal life with the Father already has begun
- A citizen of the Kingdom of God, which also is within, with authority over all the power of the enemy (Luke 10:19)

If Christians are all those things, why are so many of us failures in life? We are defeated because we do not *believe* we are all those things. We are in the position of someone with a million-dollar bank account, who will not believe he has a right to write checks on that account.

Whatever you picture can come true in your life, if you have sufficient faith in the power of God within you. You must think in terms of forever and eternity and being an heir to Jesus in order to be a success in this life. A small man is motivated by small thoughts. He cannot "think big" and remain small.

Do you lead the pack, or are you one of the pack? To be a leader in your family, your line of work, you must know how to be led by the power within you.

Here is where Saul made an obvious mistake. When he arrived home after the donkey hunt, his uncle asked where he had been, and Saul answered, "Looking for the donkeys, and when we could not find them, we went to see Samuel." (1 Sam. 10:14.)

Then the uncle naturally wanted to know what Samuel had told them. Saul simply said the prophet told them the donkeys had been found. (1 Sam. 10:15,16.) He never mentioned being anointed king. Nor did he mention meeting a procession of prophets and having the Spirit of the Lord fall on him so that he too prophesied. (1 Sam. 10:10.)

Perhaps the reason is that people who knew him made

fun of him running with the prophets. We are not told what his life as a young man had been like to cause this ridicule and astonishment. In fact, in later years, when something hard to believe occurred, "Is Saul also among the prophets?" became a common saying. (1 Sam. 10:11,12.)

It seems that, although he was a king, Saul never was able to *feel* that is who he was. He became "hung up" on who he had been before becoming king. If he had been asked who he was for quite a long time, he probably would have answered, "a son of Kish," rather than "king of Israel."

To attain true success, you must begin to think of yourself as a child of God and a follower of Jesus. A little psychological "game," which has been around for several years, may help change your thinking.

When you read, "Who are you?" write down the first thing that comes into your head. That will tell you who you *think* you are. Then you can begin to work at changing your thinking to line up with the truth of God.

In a small church, when this question was asked of the women, the answers ranged from "Jimmy's wife," to "So-and-So's daughter," to "Sue's mother." Those women had identity problems. Finally, one woman answered, "I am (and gave her name). I am me."

The pastors began to help those other women come to a realization of their true identity: whole in themselves as children of God. If you find yourself thinking of your identity in terms of your job or profession, that also is a false identity. Even in a five-fold office, a minister, for example, is not *who* you are. It is what you are called to do for God.

Who Are You?

Jesus was adamant on this point, saying, "If you don't acknowledge Me before the world, I will not acknowledge you before the Father." (Matt. 10:32.) We must "confess" that who we are is a child of God and follower of Jesus.

Saul's heart was changed by God that day with Samuel, but his nature and his ways seem never to have changed. From the beginning, he never admitted who he was *after* being anointed, until it was forced on him.

Keith Belknap of the Champions Organization, the greatest all-time achiever in the history of the Amway Corporation, wrote something pertaining to being an Amway salesperson that, in principle, applies to any situation:

> Make a public declaration. Put yourself on the line; talk your world into being; paint yourself into a corner, and make it hard to quit. Let the world laugh, but Amway put one billion, 400 million dollars in the bank (the year he said this), and has made more millionaires than any other corporation in history.[2]

Two interesting scriptures in 2 Corinthians form a faith-building pattern:

> **We boldly say what we believe . . . just as the psalm writer did when he said, "I believe and therefore I speak" (4:13 TLB).**

> **We dare to say these good things about ourselves only because of our great trust in God through Christ that he will help us to be true to what we say (3:4 TLB).**

Faith and confidence grow by alternately believing and confessing, then confessing and believing even bigger and better things. It is like climbing a ladder — step by step, alternating our feet.

There is a difference between wishing or hoping and using the faith God gave us (Rom. 12:3) to bring things to pass. When faith is challenged by trials, tribulations, and perplexities of life, we sometimes slide back into wishing or hoping that things will "work out."

Victory is not "Que sera, sera," (whatever will be will be), but it is making "whatever" actually *be* through the power and anointing of God. Fear of criticism or being made fun of will discourage you from doing the will of God. You will not be able to achieve your goal successfully.

This message I teach and write about — biblical success — upsets those who believe poverty is next to godliness. At times, I catch a lot of "flak." However, I know who I am in God, and I know my position is to teach what is sound about success in this world, consistent with the Word of God.

I do not teach success from the world's perspective, which means climbing to the top by your own strength and abilities no matter who you have to climb over on the way up. I teach that success comes from the leading of God and from applying His principles to the situations of life.

Once again, *who are you?* You are a spirit made new by God in His image, you live in a body tailored to exist in the material world, and you have a soul (mind, will, and emotions) developed since conception by your environment, education, and choice of reactions to events.

You were created and designed by God not to be moved by what you can see in the natural, but by what you know of Him and His ways. You are supposed to think in spiritual terms, not material. (2 Cor. 5:7.) God is a Spirit, and we must relate to Him in spiritual terms. (John 4:24.)

The road to the top requires a good map. I often say that life is a journey necessitating a roadmap, but most try to travel without a map or plan because they never got one in school!

Once you find out who you are, and what your position is, then you can develop real self-esteem instead of pride or a facade, a false front that will not stand up under pressure.

Once you get a revelation of, and truly believe, that you are a child of God, a member of an eternal family made up of countless brothers and sisters — all individuals but of one blood — you will find yourself with a feeling of self-worth that you never had before.

---

[1]Graham, Billy. *Storm Warning*, (Dallas: Word Publishing Co., 1992, 1995), p. 91.

[2]Belknap, Keith.

8

Develop a Sense of Self-Worth

God's mercy and grace makes "heroes" out of "zeroes."[1]
— Pulpit Helps

God has taken a "zero" and made a "hero" out of every Christian. The problem is that some of us still have identity crises. We do not know who we really are. We live like paupers when we are sons and daughters of *the* King.

Saul apparently could not believe in his own self-worth. He pulled the position of king on over his inferiority feelings and attempted to use it as a cloak to cover negative attitudes. His pride was a cover-up for fear, not a source of strength. He tried to look like a kingly person, but not be one.

God made him a "different person" on the inside (1 Sam. 10:6), but he failed to allow that to be reflected on the outside. He was like a New Testament Christian who refuses to allow the inner man to rule the outward habits, behavior, and attitudes — a Christian who still acts like a sinner.

In the end, Saul fell victim to pride, which God hates. (Prov. 8:13.) However, in my experience a thousand fail to achieve because of a lack of self-esteem for every one who achieves and then falls through pride.

It does seem as though Saul's pride covered a feeling of inferiority, however, in spite of being so impressive in appearance. Nevertheless, when Samuel told him to stop worrying about the donkeys which had been found and that he was now the desire of all Israel, Saul's response belittled himself:

> ... **"But am I not a Benjamite, from the smallest tribe of Israel, and is not my clan the least of all the clans of the tribe of Benjamin? Why do you say such a thing to me?**
>
> **1 Samuel 9:21**

That may sound like humility; however, from Saul's other actions, we know it really was a lack of self-worth speaking. Perhaps he had been lorded over by his brothers, as David's brothers did him (which did not seem to bother David — 1 Sam. 17:28,29). Perhaps his clan was poor and downtrodden by the others, although Saul's father, Kish, is called "a man of standing." (1 Sam. 9:1.)

Perhaps Benjamin's descendants, being the least in number, were treated as of less consequence than the others. At any rate, an indication of how the other Israelites felt about Saul and/or his clan can be found in 1 Samuel 10:26.

The Bible says some of them "despised" Saul, brought him no gifts when he was anointed king, and even said, "How can this fellow save us?"

For whatever reason, it seems that Saul struggled with a lack of self-esteem all of his life, and instead of becoming a winner, at the end, he failed. Someone has said a strong sense of identity may give a man an idea he can do no wrong, but too little sense of identity can produce the same result, as compensation for inferiority.

Samuel had Saul and his servant sit at the head of the table with 30 guests and gave him the choicest part of the meat, that usually kept for an honored guest. It was not the servant who protested such a high honor; it was Saul. The prophet had to insist that he eat the portion of honor. (1 Sam. 9:23,24.)

Every human being *is* a spirit (who will live forever in either heaven or hell), who lives in a body, and has an individual soul (personality, made up of mind, will, and emotion). Our Creator and Heavenly Father is a Spirit (John 4:24); therefore, we must see ourselves primarily in terms of the spirit, not the flesh.

If we *know* that we are re-born from the Adamic race into the "Jesus race," we know we have been made new creatures (new creations) in God. (2 Cor. 5:17.) Do you really think God owns or made anything without worth?

God Made No Junk

The catchy slogan, "God made no junk," may not be grammatically correct, but in principle, it is true. Our bodies are not yet perfect, of course. They exist under the handicap of heredity, a polluted environment, and the conditions of a fallen world society. However, we are not supposed to get a sense of self-worth from whether or not we have a beautiful or handsome "earth suit." Our bodies will be transformed at the Resurrection. (1 Cor. 15:51-53.)

Our souls also are not yet perfected (Eph. 3:14), being the products of all the information (true and false) and individual choices (right and wrong) we have made from the time we became aware in our mothers' wombs. The renewing of our souls by making new choices, throwing out false information, and gaining truth from Bible study (reading and hearing) is an ongoing process of sanctification. Paul called it "working out your salvation." (Philip. 2:12.)

Not understanding about spirit, soul, and body, however, causes Christians to base beliefs about themselves on appearance, education, or social status. Those things are what we do, not *who we are*. As Christians, we are children of God, unique individuals all valued equally by God, and that is where we can derive an understanding of real self-worth.

Adam and Eve were perfect until they sinned. The Bible even says Lucifer, whom we call "satan," meaning the adversary, was perfect until sin was found in him. (Ezek. 28:15 KJV; the NIV says he was "blameless.") Therefore, it is true that God created nothing imperfect or "junk." It follows, then, that when He re-creates us at salvation as "new creations," our new spirits also are perfect.

The problem is that we do not allow the inner man, recreated in the image of God, to run things all of the time. Someone without a sense of self-worth is not "in touch" with his real self. He is deceived by the enemy into looking at the outer "camouflage" of soul and body.

Your mind amasses, judges, and uses information; your emotions are how you feel about things; but, *your will is the most important factor* in your attitude, your behavior, and your success:

- When you set your will to believe what the Bible says about you — that you are worth enough to God for Him to sacrifice His Son to make a way for man's reconciliation to Him — you can have no lack of self-worth.

- When you set your will to believe a promise in God's Word that is to each and every child of His, therefore personally yours, patience grows and stamina is developed.

- When you set your will under the authority of the will of God as revealed to you by the Holy Spirit, you become strong. You can overcome whatever habit you need to stop, whatever thoughts or attitudes that need to be changed, and whatever stronghold of the enemy you need to "pull down" (carnal habits, ways of thinking, and so forth). (2 Cor. 10:4,5; Eph. 4:22; Col. 3:9 KJV.)

Men have succeeded without formal schooling, without experience, or without social status or financial backing. However, none have succeeded without *will power*.

Your will is set to fail from the beginning of any enterprise or undertaking if you do not believe you can or should win. Your will is set in negative faith, against rather than for winning. The power of failure has been loosed in your life.

There is a greater power from the spiritual realm that will work in the material, however, and that is *faith* in God, in His Word and promises, and in yourself because you are in Him. Jesus gave us authority over all the power of the enemy. (Luke 10:19.) All negative things are part of the power of the enemy.

If you do not want to be a failure, *do not accept failure as a reasonable, possible concept*. This is not to say there will not be difficulties, problems, or even trouble in this world. (John 16:33.) There are times when life seems "to throw the book" at you. The Bible says we can overcome those things and come out of them victorious — strengthened not weakened.

The Apostle James wrote:

Consider it pure joy, my brothers, whenever you face trials of many kinds, because you know that the testing of your faith develops perseverance. Perseverance must finish its work so that you may be mature and complete, not lacking anything.

James 1:2-4

The Apostle Paul also wrote about tribulations. He even said to "glory" in them. (Rom. 5:3-5 KJV.) That means to take advantage of them. It does not mean to like them, but use them to build spiritual muscles. You grow spiritually as you experience firsthand what the Word of God will do in your life.

Some victims of political or religious persecution lost everything, but came to this country, started over, and become very successful people. People with physical handicaps have become wealthy, held high positions, and/or led productive lives of service to others. Other victims of persecution or physical handicaps have chosen to remain defeated and to maintain victim mentalities, and have not lived productive, successful lives.

Failure Is a State of Mind

A mindset of failure leads to, or causes, actual failure in life. From being a state of mind, failure becomes a state of being. If you give up, you will fail to see the outcome of your plan. Through experiencing problems and developing faith and patience, your hope will increase.

It is really unworthy of a Christian to say, "Well, I've had it! This problem is too much for me."

That person is not relying on his "everpresent help in time of trouble" (Ps. 46:1) for advice and help. The Apostle Paul wrote that God always makes a way for us out of temptations and trials. (1 Cor. 10:13.) However, we must seek Him to find out what that way is.

Some say not "to be too heavenly minded to be any earthly good," but I say you *cannot* be of any earthly good until you are heavenly minded.

To follow our roadmaps to our goals, we must never admit the possibility of straying off the path. If we do inadvertently stray, we must look on it only as a detour, not a failure. We can always find the way back with God's help. Someone has remarked that there are no traffic jams on the straight and narrow way.

The successful men and women of the world never lose sight of their goals, their visions. All that is good and right can be drawn to you in life by right thinking. Faith is simply believing that something is so. Whether or not what you believe is true determines whether you operate in negative or positive faith, in a goal of failure or a goal of success.

You can accomplish anything you want in this world, providing you want it badly enough and are willing to pay the price. That entails believing in your own worth and abilities. Successful people do the things that failures are afraid to try.

Another principle of success that I have followed all my life is: Always put yourself on the spot. Tell others what your goal is, leave yourself no room to "cop out," lock all escape hatches, and move in only one direction — forward.

Proverbs 29:18 says where there is no vision, people perish. In other words, without a goal, you will fail, and you cannot have a goal without a vision, a dream. You cannot have the right vision without wisdom, and the starting point of wisdom is to trust and reverence the Lord. (Prov. 1:7.)

An affirmation to self-worth includes these steps:

1. I am created in the image of God.

2. I choose happiness and a better way to live.

3. Failure can never overtake me if my will to succeed is strong enough.

4. I will *strive* to win by:

    Starting small,
    Thinking tall,

47

Reaching over the wall of negative thoughts and habits,
Investing my all,

Visualizing what I want and what I want to be,

Expecting to get back up if I fall.

The way to overcome a lack of self-worth is to become so committed to a goal that you have no time to feel inferior. Set your focus on Jesus, not on self. Manage your destiny, or someone else will do it for you!

---

[1]*Pulpit Helps*, May 1996, p. 17.

9

Dare To Believe the Unbelievable

The only way of discovering the limits of the possible is to venture a little way past them into the impossible.[1]

— Arthur C. Clarke

In 1 Samuel 10:2-8, the prophet told Saul a sequence of things that were going to happen to him. Because Saul at that time reached beyond the things he thought were possible into the things he probably thought were impossible, he believed Samuel's words, and "God changed Saul's heart." All those things were fulfilled that day. (1 Sam. 10:9.)

We live in a time when it seems impossible things become possible every day. Things happen, both good and evil, that "boggle the mind." Nothing should surprise us anymore. However, those things are happening in the material, natural realm.

At the same time, doubt and cynicism permeate our society about things in the spiritual realm that already have been proven possible over the centuries. Yet the prevailing view is that those age-old beliefs are *not* possible and healing, miracles, and even God are myths or falsehoods.

Jesus ran into this societal mindset even in His day, particularly in His own hometown of Nazareth, where He could "do no mighty works because of their unbelief." (Matt. 13:58.)

The impossible happens to those who dare to believe the unbelievable, and the "impossible" then becomes believable to everyone else. The key to success is believing the impossible *before* it becomes possible.

> Nothing is impossible; there are ways that lead to everything, and if we had sufficient will we should always have sufficient means. — It is often merely for an excuse that we say things are impossible. . . . It is not so much (lack of) means, as perseverance, that is wanting to bring things to a successful (ending).[2]

In practical terms, the first several times I heard the Amway presentation, I left the meetings, along with most others attending, shaking my head in unbelief at the fabulous opportunities the plan offered. Yet the "impossible" story was being told by truthful people I had known for years.

Keith Belknap, whom I quoted in an earlier chapter, struggled at times to pay bills of less than $100. Yet, in four and a half years with Amway, he made in excess of $10 million.

I am encouraged by the lives of some who failed in every field, then succeeded because they never gave up. They always believed the unbelievable and refused to accept failure as final:

- One of France's greatest novelists, Emile Zola, got a zero in literature in school; now his books are "great literature." (I am not recommending his books, but they are considered classics.)

- Albert Einstein was a poor student in school, yet he had one of history's greatest scientific minds.

- Elias Howe, inventor of the cotton gin, once was homeless, jobless, and hungry. Yet he kept trying until his invention brought the equivalent of $4,000 a day in today's currency.

- Thomas Alva Edison only had three months of formal education. His father thought he was stupid, and Edison himself almost decided he was a "dunce." He was always at the foot of the class in school; however, he took refuge in the library. He did not read books, he read "the library."[3]

- John Milton, author of *Paradise Lost* and other great classics, was blind; and Beethoven, a great composer and musician, became deaf.

- George Westinghouse, inventor and founder of the electrical manufacturing company that bears his name, once was called "dull" and "backward."

- Winston Churchill, one of England's greatest prime ministers, failed his school examinations.

- Abraham Lincoln's failure to gain local, state, and national office several times is well-known.

- Dr. Von Braun, whom I quoted earlier, was the world's foremost missile and satellite expert of his time. Yet he failed math and physics in his early teens.

One man was fired from his job, then made a small fortune making and selling toys; another succeeded by selling hot dogs; and yet another had the idea of bending a piece of wire into what became paper clips. All the little things in our society that we take for granted were great ideas to someone at some time.

I could go on listing pages of people who failed, "went back to the fork in the road," and then became great successes all because they believed they could, like the little engine of the children's story, who kept saying, "I think I can! I think I can!" and climbed the grade successfully.

It Is What You Can Do That Matters

Begin your path to success by finding out what you can do and believing in it. The world pays you for what you can do, what you can give. Never mind if you cannot give what the "rich and famous" do. Find what you can do, and begin to do it.

Get other people to help you by promoting your ideas and dreams. Perhaps their goal will be to work alongside you. That seems like a small thing, but the fulfillment of big dreams and visions comes when we do not put off the little things involved in God's ultimate plan.

In addition to not trying to be a "lone ranger," we must get original ideas from God that will be the vehicle by which we reach our goals. From the numerous ideas we get every day, we should be able to sort out a few and let the Holy Spirit show us how to apply them toward the fulfillment of God's will.

Many Christians seem to think a lack of organized planning is "following the guidance of the Spirit." However, God is an orderly Being. He is not the father or author of chaos or confusion. (1 Cor. 14:33.) I see too many Christians whose main characteristics are indecision, procrastination, failure to act on ideas, lack of organization, and a compromising attitude.

However, I know that all of us are susceptible to these things, but we do not have to receive them as permanent parts of our character. When I was in college, I became impatient and indecisive, because getting through school seemed such a big obstacle. In fact, I quit many times before I really decided to settle down and persevere.

In my earlier years I was so indecisive it is painful to remember! However, I did not remain that way. I got to the place where I could believe the unbelievable. Some people believe in a day that literally will never come. That is "someday."

Instead of going to God and allowing Him to lead us toward the fulfillment of the plan or goal He has given us, many times we act like a parent assembling a child's toy. We get through the first four steps, become impatient, wad up the directions, throw them away, and give up. When we come back to finish, we must spend a lot of unnecessary time and effort trying to figure out the proper way to assemble the toy without any directions!

We must learn to hear the voice of God and follow Him step by step. Impatience leads to compromise, and compromise on wrong things at the wrong time will lead to failure.

Someone has said that we will never be happy if what we believe and what we do are two different things. Compromise has two opposite effects: It is good when necessary to make peace, to solve problems in relationships, but compromise is another word for failure if it involves right from wrong or principles.

Another common mistake is believing the impossible but not waiting on God to lead us to the destination. We then do things contrary to God's will. The Israelites made two mistakes in one situation. They refused to believe that taking the Promised Land was possible, refused to follow God one step at a time. Then the next day, after He had forbidden them to go into the land, they tried to "finish the plan" without directions.

Storming the enemy in their own power without the leadership of Moses or the will and guidance of God, many of them were killed. The nation was defeated. (Num. 14:44,45.) With God everything was possible; without God, everything was impossible.

They failed to understand what they could and could not do. The failure of that first generation of Israelites brought out of Egypt should be a lesson to us not to follow their ways, but to follow the ways of Jesus.

They were so earthly minded, focused on food and idolatry, that they had no imagination to envision the future. They even followed God's first steps of direction imperfectly, full of rebellion and disobedience to Moses and God. Then after two years of traveling toward the goal, on the very verge of success, they threw away the directions!

Let's not leave imagination out of the factors necessary for success, or we will never reach our "promised lands."

---

[1]Clarke, Arthur C. *Profiles of the Future*, (New York: Holt, Rinehart and Winston).

[2]*New Dictionary of Thoughts*, "Impossibility," pp. 296,297.

[3]*Dictionary of Quotable Definitions*, "Thomas Alva Edison (1847-1931)," p. 161.

10

Utilize the Power of Imagination

Life is like a ten-speed bike. Most of us have gears we never use.[1]

— Charles M. Schulz

Some cartoonists and comic-strip artists utilize their imaginations to bring us graphic but condensed "bites" of wisdom. One such is the man who draws "Peanuts" for United Feature Syndicate. Charles M. Schulz' quote above is very true. One of those gears many people do not use — or do not use in the right way — is *imagination.*

Saul seems to have had little positive imagination, but to have lived in the mundane. Later, as king, he "imagined" that David was trying to usurp his throne. This was a reflection of negative faith, the belief that he was not worthy.

Already, God had let Samuel know that Saul was coming to him while hunting donkeys and even where the donkeys were. Why did Saul not get the idea to go see Samuel? Could it have been his lack of imagination that hindered inspiration? Imagination is what allowed Saul's servant to come up with the idea of contacting the prophet. (1 Sam. 9:6.)

Nothing outweighs the impetus of rightly shaped imagination toward success. It is the "trigger" that sets the rocket off on its trajectory toward the target. Another wise saying is, "Anything the human mind can conceive, it can achieve." The "conceiving" part is where the imagination comes in.

Doubt and mistrust are reflections of a timid imagination. One idea from your imagination, one inspired idea from God, can build your success and, sometimes, make you a fortune. I advise spending 15 to 30 minutes a day thinking of ideas that will help you reach your dreams.

Imagination gives us hope. If you already have an idea of how to reach your goal of success, turn your imagination loose on it. Imagine every day what it will be like to achieve it. As a practical example, say that you need $10,000. Take a few minutes every day to imagine counting that money, to see yourself receiving it, and to see yourself doing whatever you have planned to do with it.

If you need a new car, see yourself driving it, washing it, admiring it, filling the tank with gas, and so forth. Do this especially just before you go to sleep and when you wake up in the morning. Great men always have known the mind is like a magnet. It attracts whatever it concentrates on.

We get out of life exactly what we put into it, nothing more. That is an old folk-saying, but it is true. When we put good thoughts, constructive efforts, and hard work into life, we succeed. What we sow, we will reap, good or bad. (Gal. 6:7.)

What you imagine must be backed by faith in God and faith in yourself, however, or imagining becomes simply "day-dreaming." The power of imagination can be deflected, or negated, by always visualizing your dream, but never doing anything about it. It can also be smothered by looking at circumstances, which can cause you to disbelieve in the possible, much less the impossible!

That is what happened to the Israelites. It is very easy to let circumstances cause your imagination to turn negative, which is what happened to Saul.

An optimist is one who always imagines the best.

A pessimist is one who always imagines the worst.

An optimistic pessimist is one who says, "I never believe things can turn out quite as bad as I think they are going to!"

Which category do you fall into? You will succeed quicker by turning into an optimist, if you are not one already. Christians ought to be optimists by nature. We know we have already won through Jesus. No matter how bad things look in the world at one time or another, we *know* God's purpose and plan is intact and progressing inexorably toward victory.

Positive imagining, or optimistic thinking, keeps us from embarrassment. How can we be ashamed along the way, if we know the present problem is just another obstacle to overcome on the way to victory?

You Cannot Soar Too High on Your Own Wings

If the idea is your own, confirmed or given by God, you need not fear failure. It is true that "the higher you climb, the harder you fall" — unless you are fastened very strongly to the mountain you are climbing. Our "Mountain" is Jesus. However, without the "wings" of imagination, you will never get off the ground.

Carl Sagan wrote in his book, *Cosmos*:

Imagination will often carry us to worlds that never were. But without it, we go nowhere.[2]

Without imagination, we would not be able to believe in God — which is why He created it within man. Without imagination, Abraham never would have expected to have a

57

son in his old age. Vision begins with imagination, and faith follows vision.

I have learned not to look at things I see in the natural.

I have learned not to believe in circumstances.

I have learned not to accept failure as anything but temporary. Some people fail once and spend the rest of their lives hanging their heads in shame when they could get up and try again, more than likely bringing victory out of defeat.

By exercising patience, using our imaginations to instill us with hope, engaging in spiritual warfare, and speaking forth the word of faith as we do what our hands find to do, we can see God's will for us become reality.

We need to "get up" off our beds of ease and be about the Master's business. Someone has said the ships that come in while we sit and wait are usually "hardships." Spend your time looking for road signs to the goal, not those which point the other way.

---

[1]Quoted in *Reader's Digest*, "Quotable Quotes."

[2]Sagan, Carl. *Cosmos*, (New York: Random House).

11

Look for Signs of Success, Not Failure

(Failure is) the highway to success, inasmuch as every discovery of what is false leads us to seek . . . after what is true.[1]

– John Keats

Saul quite early in his life as king faced a tremendous opposing army of Philistines. Neither he nor any of his army looked for success in that venture. All looked for failure and expected defeat. However, one young shepherd lad came along and refused to see failure. (1 Sam. 17.)

All David saw was success in the future and success in his past when he killed a bear and a lion. (1 Sam. 17:34-37.) He defeated the enemy's giant champion with a slingshot and won the battle for Israel. His main premise of operation was: "God is on Israel's side, so how can we lose?" (1 Sam. 17:6.)

We desperately need to remember that God is on *our* side, so how can we lose?

Americans seem to satisfy any yearning for change by following fads, but remain "stick-in-the-muds" where change

59

in tradition is concerned. There was good advice in the old poem that advised not to be the first "by whom the new is tried," nor yet "the last to lay the old aside."

When the first paganistic ideas began to circulate in this country — evolution, humanism, socialism, Eastern religions, there-is-no-God — most people laughed or scorned them. After all, we were a Christian nation, founded on biblical principles.

However, very subtly, the people whom satan used to promulgate his anti-God and anti-Christ ideas gradually sowed more and more seed. Finally, today, we are reaping a harvest of wickedness because of complacency, both in government and in our home lives.

What happened? The Church stopped being an example and allowed itself to be relegated to "religion." Christians became ashamed of prosperity, especially in the 1980s when a few ministries which had grossly misused their resources had the rug pulled out from under them.

The gospel cannot be taken to the ends of the earth and all nations made disciples of Jesus without money. (Matt. 28:19 NIV.) To complete the Great Commission, God's people *must* prosper. The motive in getting wealth must be right: to distribute what God has given us as good stewards of His supply.

We must begin to prosper individually in order that the Church may prosper as a Body. We must begin to get in position to lead the world to the old ways of spiritual tried and true paths of righteousness in God, eternal truths that are never outdated.

This is what the Lord says: Stand at the crossroads and look; ask for the ancient paths, ask where the good way is, and walk in it, and you will find rest for your souls.

Jeremiah 6:16

To take the right path at a "crossroads," we must look at signposts of success. If we look at the signs of failure — which are more prevalent in society today than success — we will never turn this country around. The same is true in your personal life. Could reading this book mark a crossroad for you?

Life is not easy, especially as a Christian living in a pagan nation. You need to examine very carefully what you read, what movies you watch, and especially what television programs you see. Nearly every program promotes at least one concept that is a "sign of failure" to the Church. The old-time script writers who at least had their roots in Christian thinking and were genuine literary people are dead or retired in old age.

However, the majority of today's national news media personnel, script writers, directors, and producers are atheists or agnostics, studies show. Nearly all newscasts are biased toward the secular world view of the writers, reporters, or network heads. The same is true of newspapers and magazines. It is a rare television program that does not have at least one underlying "message" that is immoral, unethical, or even illegal.

Therefore, if the Church is to prosper, we must not look at signs of failure, but at signs of success: great revivals, more souls being saved worldwide than at any other time, more people joining or attending Full Gospel churches, although mainline churches are losing members.

Life is not easy today, in spite of living in one of the greatest general prosperity periods in our history. Everyone has some hardships, sorrow, economic difficulty, or other problem to face. However, the people who find God have access to the ability to gain victory over anything life brings.

It's Not Over Till It's Over

What is true in our Church and national life is just as true for individuals: *Look for and at signs of success, not failure.*

61

The old saying, "It's not over till the fat lady sings," is still true in principle.[2]

This natural life is not over for you until it is over, and you have passed into the next life. The reason adages become adages is because most of them are eternal truths. For example: "Where there is life, there is hope." Suppose you have "failed" at marriage, parenting, business, or a career? That is not the end. Look on it as a challenge, an obstacle, a trial that is perfecting your patience.

Sit down with a "re-organization plan" and find out what went wrong and what was right. Look primarily for signs of success. It is most important to lay aside blame, or you will not see straight. Do not blame others, do not blame yourself, and above all things, do not blame God!

Evangelist-author-pastor David Wilkerson wrote in a recent news letter that God had been dealing very strongly with him about a "grievous sin" God's people have fallen into that fosters doubt and disbelief. Wilkerson wrote that the Holy Spirit spoke these words to him:

> When sudden calamity falls, and (My people) face
> fear, trouble, poverty — the heart always questions,
> "Why is life so hard when I only do what is right?"
> That is exactly the time when they are on the brink
> of a terrible abyss. They are on the verge of indulging
> in a sin that is ruinous![3]

Wilkerson said the sin is charging God with neglect and injustice. We are impugning God's character when we blame Him for things that happen.

I was so pleased to hear that the governor of Arkansas, Michael Huckaby, would not sign a victim relief bill in 1997, because it attributed a major tornado disaster to "an act of God."

Arkansas legislators agreed to delete those words. That was the act of a courageous Christian.

Successful people never whine and sit around assigning blame for seeming failures or setbacks. That is what the Israelites did on the journey from Egypt. Ten times they grumbled, complained, and blamed God because they did not have what they wanted or because the journey seemed difficult. As a consequence, they were not allowed to enter the Promised Land. (Num. 14:22.)

Are American Christians on the verge of judgment over this sin?

Are you guilty of this? Please stop blaming God for anything. He loves you. (John 3:16.) He means good for you and not evil. (Jer. 29:11.) There are reasons for what happens that you may never know in this life, but you can "take it to the bank" that God did not cause bad things to happen in your life.

There has been entirely too much discussion in recent years about "why bad things happen to good people." There are three general and simple reasons for this without going into individual circumstances:

1. We live in a battle zone where fallout is common and bad things happen to everyone, just as the rain falls on "the just and the unjust." (Matt. 5:45.)

2. All cultures, religions, economics, politics, and other social systems are under the authority and influence of the "prince of this world" (order, or society) — our adversary. (John 12:31, 14:30, 16:11.) When Jesus returns, He is not going to "fix" or "renovate" *any* of the world's present systems but replace them with God's systems. (To know what they are, read the Bible).

3. We probably are living in the winding up of all earthly history, whether it is five or 50 years, or longer. The war

was won by Jesus on the cross (Col. 2:14), but the final battles between the Body of Christ and "guerrillas" (demonic forces) are accelerating in frequency and intensity. Before long, the remaining enemy forces are going to be "kicked out," given eternal prison sentences, and confined to a lake of fire. (Rev. 20:11-15.)

In the meantime, we need to "get on with occupying the territory until Jesus returns." (Luke 19:13.) To do that, we must succeed in life in all areas. Achievers look for signs of success and find them!

Never accept failure. Nine times out of ten, on the other side of what seems a failure is success. The secret of living life victoriously is how close your fellowship is to Jesus and how well you obey the Holy Spirit. The closer you walk to the Godhead, the more immunity you have to failure. (Ps. 91.) You will never be immune from difficulty, however.

A Man Who Refused To Fail

My weekly radio show, "Who Said That?" on a Tulsa station generates quite a bit of mail. Not long ago, I received a letter from a man who is a great example of someone going through "bad things," but refusing to fail.

Dear Dr. Leding:

I am 56 years young. I have been married 31 years. I had a son. He was killed in an auto accident at 18. Recently, my wife wanted her freedom, which I gave her without bitterness or resentment, in spite of the fact that nearly everything I had worked for was being taken from me. I valued the experience enough not to let my peace of mind be disturbed.

Our lives were so interwoven that I thought it would be easier to forget the past if I started life anew somewhere else, as I try always to look forward to something better. The lessons I learned are priceless, so I really have no regrets. What I lost materially, I gained spiritually, and no one can take that from me. I found peace and contentment within.

It wasn't easy to give up my son or my wife, my home, or my friends, but I found that security is within oneself and not in persons, places, or things. We really do not possess anything except in our own consciousnesses (minds). Life is a challenge, but that is what makes it interesting. I am in love with it. I feel more alive now than before I gave up so much.

By disciplining and controlling my thoughts, I create harmony in my life, and thank heaven, no one can control that but me! So I cannot blame anyone but myself if I am not happy. Now I am grateful for my problems. Adversities are really stepping stones to something better. The more I study the Bible, the more the mysteries of life unfold to me. Sometimes I feel like I will burst with joy.

Is that not a story of success? Like the man who wrote that letter, if you will think, "I will not accept this as defeat," when the going gets rough, then all the resources of Heaven will flow toward you to bring victory. (Philip. 4:13.)

Someone has said it does not matter how many times you get knocked down, it is how many times you get up that counts. Let go of your past mistakes and move on.

---

[1]*Webster's Dictionary of Quotable Definitions*, "Failure," p. 189.

[2]A reference to the late, great singer Kate Smith who used to be guest artist at the conclusion of games and competitions.

[3]Wilkerson, David. *Times Square Church Pulpit Series*, "I Almost Slipped!" (Lindale, TX: World Challenge, Inc., 3/7/97), p. 2.

12

Let the Past *Be* the Past

One problem with gazing too frequently into the past is that we may turn around to find the future has run out on us.[1]

—Michael Cibenko

When a would-be achiever sets out to reach a goal, he must do two things: Set his eyes on the future with faith and patience, and let go of the remorse and condemnation associated with problems or events of his past life.

Saul never let the past be the past. He developed a tendency to brood, to get into dark depressed moods. He imagined David was trying to steal his throne and, no matter what happened and how much he was proved wrong, he never let go of past mistakes, but kept repeating them.

The part of human nature that wants to grieve and mourn over the past shows up in as simple a thing as salesmen's orders. Most salesmen fear and hate the cancellation of an order after enduring more than a dozen turn-downs before writing the order. I personally have found myself grumbling over a canceled order longer than it would have taken to sell five new ones — thereby losing all six!

Amaziah, another of David's descendants who was king of Judah, once spent 100 talents of silver (about 3.75 tons) to hire mercenaries from the nation of Israel to fight with his army against the Arameans (present-day Syria). (2 Chron. 25:6.)

By the way, a *talent* in the Bible is money, not an "ability" or "gift" as we define it today. When Jesus told of the wicked servants who "buried" their talents, He was saying they did not use the money given them to add to His Kingdom. The "good and faithful" servants were those who obediently invested money to make more for the Master. (Matt. 25:14-30.)

As Amaziah ruled during a time when Israel was given over to idolatry and rebellion and only Judah remained faithful to God, he was given a word from a "man of God" after he had hired the soldiers:

> **"O king, these troops from Israel must not march with you, for the Lord is not with Israel — not with any of the people of Ephraim. Even if you go and fight courageously in battle, God will overthrow you before the enemy, for God has the power to help or to overthrow."**
>
> **2 Chronicles 25:7**

Instead of "letting the past be the past," writing off the money as the consequences of getting ahead of (or neglecting to ask) God, the first words out of the king's mouth were, "But what will I do about the money?" (2 Chron. 25:9a.)

The man of God answered, **The Lord is able to give you much more than that!** (2 Chron. 25:9b).

To let go of that kind of mistake takes more faith than most of us possess. Yet, that is exactly what we must do if we are to go on and win the battle. The day comes for nearly every Christian when he or she needs to follow the advice expressed by Dr. Robert Schuller: "Don't look at what you have lost, but at what you have left."[2]

Even secularists and noted atheists are wiser than we are sometimes as Christians, as Jesus pointed out:

> **. . . For the people of this world are more shrewd in dealing with their own kind than are the people of the light.**
>
> **Luke 16:8**

Aldous Huxley, noted author of *Brave New World*, whose portrayal of a potentially dreadful governmental system does not seem so farfetched now as it did in 1932, wrote in the foreword to that book:

> Chronic remorse, as all the moralists are agreed, is a most undesirable sentiment. If you have behaved badly, repent, make what amends you can, and address yourself to the task of behaving better next time. On no account, brood over your wrongdoing.[3]

A simpler way of saying this is that "rolling in the muck" is not the best way to get clean! Also, a proverb puts this truth very graphically: *You cannot grind today's grain with water that flowed by the mill yesterday.*

Another man said it is futile to continue to talk over and try to "fix" the past, "something like trying to make birth control retroactive."

Two of Jesus' disciples exemplify the choices we have concerning mistakes we have made:

- Peter repented of denying Jesus during His trial for blasphemy, then "let the past be the past," and became a great apostle. (Matt. 26:69-75.)

- Judas experienced great remorse after betraying Jesus, but did not repent. He judged himself, sentenced himself, and carried out his own execution. (Matt. 27:3-5.)

Remorse will kill you; true repentance saves.

Godly sorrow brings repentance that leads to salvation and leaves no regret, but worldly sorrow (remorse) brings death.
2 Corinthians 7:10

Repent of anything you ought to, put it under the blood, and it will leave no residue of grief or remorse.

For Success in God, Give Up *All* of the Past

When I say, "Let the past be the past," I am not just talking about forgetting past mistakes as over and done with, repented of, and under the blood with no shame or condemnation attached. (Rom. 8:1.) I also mean that sometimes we must set aside the things in our pasts that have seemed good.

The Apostle Paul wrote that he had put aside everything in his past, counting it all as worth nothing, in order to gain Christ and the only successful future there is: eternity with God. He was not yet "perfected," not yet all he should or would be. However, he was "forgetting the past" and "looking forward to what lies ahead," striving to reach the end of the race and the prize waiting for him. (Philip. 3:8-15.)

The good things of Egypt became a stumbling block to the Israelites. They wanted out of slavery, but they did not want to undergo hardships on the way to a better life. They wanted the "flesh pots" and pleasures of the past.

It is harder sometimes to let go of a past that has been pleasant, fun, and seemingly good than it is to let go of a negative past full of sins and mistakes. Yet carrying either along with you can result in "weights attached to your feet," things that will cause you to be discontented with present circumstances or set you up to fail.

The theology you need to base your future as a Christian on is very simple:

1. Take time to pray, knowing that He will hear you, if what you want is in agreement with His will. (1 John 5:14.)

2. Have confidence; or believe in your heart that you can have what you desire (have faith). (Mark 11:23,24.)

3. Love what you do, put your whole heart in it, and you will deliver more than you think possible.

However, if "mental confidence" is what you are depending on, it will not get you very far. You can "confess" all day long that you can do anything, but if you do not have unshakable confidence in God's promises in your heart, your words are dropping to the floor.

Faith, or confidence, does not comes by hearing and believing the Word of God. (Rom. 10:17.) Books such as this one can help clarify your thinking, give you ideas, and help you see your mistakes. However, all of the "positive thinking" books in the world will not give you confidence to succeed. Only God's Word will do that.

An important key to success is knowing firsthand that God is a rewarder of those who seek Him diligently. (Heb. 11:6.)

If you are at the point of wondering what God wants you to have, simply pray and ask Him to show you. God may not speak to you in the clear thought David Wilkerson wrote of, but He will let you know His answer in some way.

Perhaps it will be a verse from the Bible that contains your answer, perhaps a "witness" to your heart, perhaps it will be as to Elijah, "a still, small voice" (1 Kings 19:12), or perhaps He will speak to you through other people. I am not referring necessarily to a word of prophecy. One minister reported passing two strangers carrying on a conversation. The words one of them said was her answer.

God is a Being who likes variety, but who never changes in Himself. (Mal. 3:6; Heb. 13:8.) He seems to enjoy not allowing us to "put Him in a box," or limit Him in any way. Your answer might come in a letter about something else entirely. The key is to remain alert and *expect* to receive an answer. *Trust* God, because you "know that you know" He will not leave you without guidance.

When you let go of the past and turn your eyes toward the future, make certain not to pass up any opportunity on the way. Look at every possibility like an avid fisherman turning over rocks to find exactly the right bait.

L. Frank Baum, author of the classic children's book, *The Wizard of Oz*, failed at about everything he tried to do. Then one more possibility occurred to him — writing a children's book. He wrote:

> When I was young, I longed to write a great novel that should win me fame. Now that I am getting old, my first book is written to amuse children. . . . to please a child is a sweet and lovely thing that warms one's heart.[4]

Baum changed his goal by changing his motivation. Instead of fame, he only wanted to please children while instilling these lessons:

1. What you have is usually better than a fairy-tale place at the end of a rainbow.

2. Tragedies like tornadoes can be blessings, showing you what is important in life.

If you have tried and tried and not been able to reach your goal, perhaps you have not failed — you have just been trying to reach the wrong goal. Look at what you *can* do and set another goal.

72

Do not give up without exhausting every possibility.

---

[1]"Quotable Quotes," *Reader's Digest*, May 1997, p. 37.

[2]Schuller, Dr. Robert.

[3]Huxley, Aldous. *Brave New World*, (New York: Harper & Row, 1932, 1946), p. vii.

[4]*A Sense of History*, p. 493, "The Father of Oz," by Daniel P. Mannix.

13

Exhaust Every Possibility

No one has ever really failed until he has done absolutely everything possible before he quits in the last minute of the last day of his life.

When Saul and his servant had searched five separate areas and were hungry, tired, and almost broke, Saul said in discouragement, "Let's go home. We have failed in our quest."

However, his servant realized they had not exhausted every possibility. There was still the prophet, and he lived not far from where they were. It was possible to do something more.

The late author Pearl S. Buck, daughter of missionaries to China, said:

> All things are possible until they are proven impossible — and even the impossible may only be so as of now.[1]

Even experts may be willing to give up too soon. Jesus' disciples, expert fishermen, had fished all night and caught nothing. They thought they had failed on this trip and were ready to give up. Then Jesus passed by and suggested two possibilities they had not thought about (Luke 5:4-7; John 21:6): 1) Throw the net on the other side of the boat; and 2) trying in the daylight. They had been fishing in the dark.

Reluctantly, they explored the possibility He suggested, and caught more fish than they could bring in. What apparently had been impossible last night on one side of the boat was possible the next morning on the other side of the boat.

The Bible has many stories that could illustrate this principle, but two come to mind immediately: Joshua led the Israelites around Jericho *seven* days and 13 times before the walls came down (Josh. 6), and Elijah prayed for rain *seven* times before he saw "a little cloud the size of a man's hand" and knew rain was on the way. (1 Kings 18:41-46.)

Suppose Joshua had given up before the seventh day? Suppose Elijah had prayed six times and quit? You say, "Yes, but God had told them what to do." Well, God will also tell you what to do. Too often, we think we did not hear God, and we give up before gaining victory. If God has given you a goal and led you toward it, do not give up, no matter how many times it takes.

The way to find out if you have exhausted every possibility is to pray for wisdom, analyze the situation, then meditate calmly concerning possibilities that you have not yet seen or tried. Albert Einstein said that no problem can be solved without someone continuing to think about it.

In the Christian life, meditation is a vital key to success. If we meditate — let the Word roll around in our spirits — we can deal wisely in the affairs of life. Then we will have success in whatever we do. (Josh. 1:6-8; Ps. 1,2,3.)

Do not ever ask for hardships or bring them upon yourself by behaving foolishly, but do be prepared at times to have struggles and to face difficulties. Those are the times when you need to be doublechecking for possibilities you may have missed.

Someone who truly thinks positively does not shut his eyes to trouble, nor is he afraid of it. He knows that, through the grace of God, he has the strength to cope with it. He is mature in his knowledge that there are failures along the way to success, but he is not going to dwell on the failures except to analyze them.

Victory Out of Defeat

I have met many people who have come out of a dark tunnel of struggle through faith and emerged into the light successfully. One of my wonderful Christian businessmen friends at the height of his success felt a need to give back to his community. Getting a great deal of joy out of his volunteer efforts, he brought in a young man to oversee his business.

Being a naturally generous man, he promised his new partner a sizable share of the profits. In spite of this, my friend woke up one morning to find that his "partner" had swindled him out of a lot of money. As a result, he lost his business. My friend accepted this turn of events as just one more incident in a long business career. He told me that he intended to "pray the misfortune through," knowing he would get an answer from God.

Instead of looking at failure, he looked at past successes, saying, "Just think how much more experience and know-how I have now than I did when I started 25 years ago."

He began another business, which since then has been built into another success. His mature Christian outlook regarding troubles and struggle proved to me that it truly is not what happens to us that matters, but what we do about it. My friend had developed patience and persistence during his years of experience that stood him in good stead in this crisis.

Once I became so troubled over seeing how many Christians were not receiving God's blessings that I sought the Lord as to why. The Lord told me one of the major reasons was a lack of patience and persistence. People with those characteristics have an understanding of God which those who expect instant results do not. They understand God is not a "magician" who snaps His fingers and causes things to happen with no effort on our parts.

These people are the successful ones who allow the Lord time enough to work things out and bring the scriptural promises into reality. People who have complete trust in the Lord will keep believing and standing in faith until the manifestation comes, no matter how long it takes.

Patience is an aspect, or facet, of self-control, an outgrowth of self-discipline. It means being steadfast, unmovable, stabilized in your emotions, always the same regardless of circumstances. Impatient people are up and down in their emotions, constantly undergoing "mood swings."

Persistence is a steady, continuous plodding forward toward a certain goal, with no faltering, no turning from side to side, and no stopping to take a break. Persistent people do not waver in faith. allow circumstances to control them, or follow wrong influences that steer them off course. They walk forward in the face of opposition, endure persecution, and are longsuffering.

The writer of Hebrews challenged Christians to not "cast away" their confidence. (Heb. 10:35,36.) In other words, do not give up. When the Word is at work in your life, you must have patience for it to produce. You must believe that God will watch over His Word to perform it. (Jer. 1:12; Ps. 119:106.)

When dreams and visions are challenged by the perplexities of life, only patience enables you not to become angry or discouraged. Patience, persistence, and one more characteristic — tenacity — will get you past the attacks of the enemy designed to pull you off the track, cause you to lose sight of your goal, or cause you to "throw in the towel" and forfeit the match.

The test of character that leads to success is whether or not you are a "bulldog" when doing the right thing and when achieving God's will for you.

"Hanging on" or "digging in one's heels" is *tenacity* when it is in aid of right things. It is *stubbornness* when it backs up self-will, pride, or rebellion. Both words mean setting your will in agreement with something outside of yourself, grabbing hold of that thing like a bulldog, and refusing to be shaken loose.

Are you tenacious or apathetic? The late great prime minister of England, Winston Churchill, once said the nose of the bulldog is slanted so he can hang on and still breathe. That is persistence, patience, and tenacity.

I like a "bulldog Christian," a person who, when God shows him something, will fasten his "jaws" into it and not let go. When I first entered the insurance business, I made a call on the owner of a clothing store, who appeared to be a successful man.

I asked him, "Sir, if you were about to depart from this earth and had met a young man who wanted to be successful, what words of wisdom could you give him?"

He thought for a moment, then said, "Persistence, persistence, persistence, persistence! That is the one thing I have learned over the years and continue to live by."

Are you up one day and down the next? Make a quality decision every day that you will not be swayed by how you feel or by what other people think and say about what you are doing.

If we had no other examples, the heroes and heroines of the Bible provide them. The writer of Hebrews gave us a list of Old Testament men and women of faith (Heb. 11), all characterized as successful in running the race even if they did not reach their goals. All had patience, persistence, and tenacity.

The "inventor of American salesmanship" is an American example of nearly everything I present in this book. Although his name is not as well-known as Henry Ford, Thomas A. Edison, or Albert Einstein, James Patterson nevertheless had a tremendous influence on modern economics and the way things are marketed.

He Refused To Be Defeated

Patterson was a former Ohio farm boy who saw an interesting-looking device of wheels and springs housed in an ornate case, a device that rang a bell when a drawer was opened. To everyone else who saw it, the machine was an object of scorn and ridicule.

However, in 1884, already past 40 with little money and several failures behind him, Patterson believed he had found his destiny. His goal became to get one of the devices in every store. He bought the rights to the cash register from its inventor, James S. Ritty, who called his machine, "Ritty's Incorruptible Cashier."

In the face of general "horse laughs," what Patterson did with the cash register, first manufactured in a slum area of Dayton, Ohio, "made entrepreneurial history." However, he had to invent American salesmanship to do it![2] One historian wrote:

> The tales told of the man himself will be repeated, with no embellishment needed, as long as men wearing name tags convene to learn how to sell widgets, or management types gather at country clubs to relax at the 19th hole.[3]

Patterson encountered difficulties, but he caught hold of his dream like a bulldog and refused to let go, overlooking no possibilities in his efforts to sell the machine. Ritty was a saloon owner, who invented the machine to cut down petty pilfering in his establishment. Naturally, many bartenders and cashiers resented and even hated this "newfangled" register.

In fact, Patterson stumbled on the invention after he discovered that his business had not turned a profit because his own clerks were dishonest. For a long time, the cash register was known as a "thief catcher." His imaginative ideas included many that we take for granted in manufacturing and selling today, even something so simple as establishing sales quotas.

The founder of the National Cash Register Company is a classic example of what I am outlining in this book: One of his favorite exhortations to his workers was, "Visualize! Analyze! Dramatize!" He had hundreds of blackboards and pads of paper provided in his plants for jotting down problems or plans.

If a foreman said he was satisfied with his work, Patterson fired him. Some of his antics were "off the wall" and not successful, but even being charged for violations of the Sherman Antitrust Act did not defeat him. He looked at his successes, not his mistakes, and he persisted.

"With his unconquerable spirit and the material resources he provided, Patterson saved the city" with a relief plan quickly drawn on his ever-present pad after the great Dayton Flood in 1913.[4] Miss Evangeline Booth, commander-in-chief of the Salvation Army, called him the "instrument of the Lord," and the legal judgments against him were dismissed in a court of appeals.

He was persistent and patient, he dreamed big dreams and refused to admit failure, and he helped others as he made his own way to the goal. He certainly used his imagination in productive ways.

> Patterson showed the way to introduce not only "big ticket" merchandise . . . but all products that require sampling and demonstration. To every doorbell

ringer of the 2,700 companies whose salesmen make five million calls every working day . . . some of Patterson's shrewd, practical psychology has been passed down.[5]

The late Calvin Coolidge, 30th President of the United States, once said:

Nothing in the world can take the place of persistence. Talent will not: nothing is more common than unsuccessful men with talent. Genius will not; the world is full of educated derelicts. Persistence and determination are (all powerful).[6]

Difficulties ("failures") can make you bitter, mean, and frustrated, or life's trials can be turned into your greatest triumphs. You must take control of your emotions and thoughts and set your will to see no situation as hopeless. Then, it is up to you and God.

---

[1]Buck, Pearl S.

[2]*A Sense of History*, p. 418, "The Machine That Kept Them Honest," by Gerald Carson.

[3]Ibid.

[4]Ibid, p. 427.

[5]Ibid, p. 429.

[6]Calvin Coolidge.

14

See No Situation as Hopeless

Someone full of faith in God and himself is the true optimist, one who sees no situation as hopeless, one who makes the most of all that comes and the least of all that goes.

Saul began his duties as king in the right way. He ignored those troublemakers who would not respect and honor him, and he refused to see the situation of the Israelites as hopeless. Besieged and afflicted by the Ammonites, the town of Gilead felt hopeless.

They had offered to surrender to the chief of the Ammonites and be his subjects; however, that ruler operated in the cruelty of pagans who know no compassion. His terms were that he would make a treaty with them only if they had their right eyes gouged out, bringing "disgrace on all Israel." (1 Sam. 11:1,2.)

The elders of the town asked for seven days to try to find a champion, or rescuer, before surrendering. Being so sure none could be found, the Ammonite chief agreed. However, during their search for someone to come to their aid, the messengers visited Saul's town.

As he ought to have been doing, Saul was plowing his fields behind his oxen, not expecting everyone to wait on him and support him because he was king. Hearing the people mourning and weeping, he asked what was the matter. When he heard, he did not consider things hopeless but "burned with anger" on behalf of the helpless people and the honor of Israel. (1 Sam. 11:5,6.)

At that point, the Spirit of the Lord came upon him. He cut his oxen into pieces, sending the pieces throughout Israel, prophesying that this would happen to the oxen of anyone who did not rally to him in defense of Jabesh Gilead. (1 Sam. 11:7.)

When you refuse to accept situations as hopeless, you can win. Saul drew 330,000 fighting men through his actions, and during the night, they broke into the Ammonite camp and slaughtered the enemy.

Then the people wanted to kill those troublemakers who had questioned Saul's ability and right to rule over them, but again Saul did the right thing: He had mercy, not vengeance, in victory. He made no effort to "get even" (1 Sam. 11:12,13), and gave all the credit to God. Then Samuel reaffirmed his kingship, and there was a great celebration.

If you are not received at first for who you are, make certain you are on God's side, and He will vindicate and promote you. (Ps. 75:6.) However, if you begin to see any situation as hopeless, you will fail in the end because you will not act.

Many successful people have been in seemingly hopeless situations, but refused to give up. Their situations may have looked hopeless to everyone else, but not to them. I have mentioned some of these people earlier in the book. Here are some other examples:

Dale Carnegie submitted his book to 16 publishers, all of whom rejected it, but he refused to accept the situation as hopeless. A publisher finally took a chance on his manuscript. Today, his well-known *How To Win Friends and Influence People* has sold more than five million copies, one of the all-time international best-sellers.[1]

A famous statesman once said:

The great difference between men, the feeble and the powerful, the great and the significant and the insignificant, is energy and determination — a purpose once fixed, and then — death or victory.

Noah Webster worked on his dictionary for 36 years; the Greek poet Virgil took 12 years to write the literary classic, *The Aeneid*; and, Britisher Edward Gibbon spent 20 years researching and writing *The Decline and Fall of the Roman Empire,*[2] one of the most prestigious histories in the world.

Someone has said that the world gives way to the man who is so determined to get what he wants that he "burns his bridges," leaving no way for retreat, and says, "I must win — or perish!"

Edison made more than 10,000 unsuccessful experiments before he developed his storage battery. Men with lesser determination would have given up long before.

Determination Puts "Feet" To Hope

Not only must you not see a situation as hopeless, but you must be determined to turn that situation around. Hope must become faith, the knowledge that what is hoped for can become reality. (Heb. 11:1.)

In spite of God's allowing him to reign 42 years, and in spite of Saul's beginning with a lot of the right acts, nowhere in the Bible do we see evidence that Saul had the determination to serve God and the people which would have allowed his posterity to inherit the throne.

Saul had determination to finish certain tasks, to do certain jobs, and he was successful *as long as he was on God's side.* Determination in an undertaking that is against God's will avail nothing; it simply becomes stubbornness. So the key to not misplacing your will and determination to win is to first make sure you are on the right track.

If you want God on your side, be sure that you are on *His* side. When things look hopeless, go to God first, then to someone whom you know will encourage you.

I like the inspiring story of a group of war refugees who escaped by traveling over very rough terrain. It seemed doubtful whether a mother and her little girl could make it. Yet they could not in good conscience leave them behind, so they agreed that the strong men would carry the child.

After three days, the path became even more difficult and steep. Finally, an old man collapsed, begging them to go on without him, to leave him and save themselves. The group sadly started onward, then the mother of the little girl suddenly took the child by the hand and walked back to the old man.

She gently placed her daughter in the old man's arms, and calmly said, "You can't quit now. It's your turn to carry my child."

Then she turned and followed the group of refugees. A few minutes later, they looked back to see the old man determinedly climbing the path behind them with the little girl in his arms.[3] All he had needed was a little encouragement, a challenge to keep trying, a reason to set his determined will toward the goal.

Perhaps the one man we can read about who had a right to think things were hopeless was Job, the wealthy man in the Middle East, whose story is the oldest book in the Bible. Job lost all his wealth, his family, his animals, and his health.

Then three friends lectured him about self-righteousness! (Job 11-31.)

His wife not only left him but urged him to curse God and die. (Job 2:9.) Job cursed the day of his birth, as he sat in the ash heap (garbage dump) scratching his boils with a broken piece of pottery, but he never cursed God. Job did justify himself rather than God with questions he wanted to ask God, but he never blamed God.

Then came a fourth friend, Elihu, who listened to all this and became angry at Job for justifying himself and at the three friends for condemning Job but not defending God. He spoke on behalf of God and how wonderful He was. (Job 32-37.)

Because Job never threw up his hands, and said, "It's hopeless. I'll just go on and die," the situation was turned for his good in the end. Also, in the first two chapters of Job, we see that God did not do those bad things to Job. He simply allowed Job to be tested in areas where he had fear. (Job. 3:25.) Fear can knock great holes in your spiritual protection "hedge."

The interesting thing is that, when God finally did speak to Job after the men had been reminded by Elihu of His goodness and grandeur and been called to worship Him, He never explained a word about why such "bad things had happened" to a good man.

Instead, the last five chapters of Job are taken up with God talking about what He had done in creation! In other words, when a situation seems hopeless, praise God, and remind yourself of His greatness, repent for any doubt or unbelief, and then set your will to wait until the situation is turned for your good.

Job was delivered from his sufferings and restored, not only to his former position of prosperity and honor but to greater blessings than he had previously received. (Job 42:12.)

Job also has the honor of being the human being who proved God right in a debate with the devil and in spite of everything Satan did.

Patience, perseverance, and determination helped Job hold out until victory came. Somehow, he never lost hope. Well-known author/pastor Charles R. Swindoll put it this way in a recent book:

> Hope is something as important to us as water is to a fish, as vital as electricity is to a light bulb, as essential as air is to a jumbo jet . . . . We cannot stay on the *road to anticipated dreams* without it . . . . Take away our hope, and our world is reduced to something between depression and despair.[4]

[1]Carnegie, Dale. *How To Win Friends and Influence People*, (New York: Simon & Schuster, 1936).

[2]Gibbon, Edward. *The Decline and Fall of the Roman Empire*, (New York: Harcourt, Brace, and Co., 1960; orig. pub. around 1776 in England).

[3]Kopmeyer, M.R.

[4]Swindoll, Charles R. *Hope Again*, (Dallas: Word Publishing, 1996), p. 3.

15

Find a Need and Fill It

The road to success is not to be run upon by seven-league boots. Step by step, little by little, bit by bit, that is the way to wealth, that is the way to wisdom, that is the way to glory.[1]

– Charles Buxton

Most of the successful people we have talked about became that way by seeing a specific need in society and inventing or devising or manufacturing something to fill it. Hence, the adage, "Necessity is the mother of invention." Mark Twain put it that necessity is the mother of taking risks.

There can be no jobs in our economy that do not somehow have the assignment of filling a need. From workers in service industries to the President of the United States, all fill a need. Even Saul was anointed king only because he was the man God picked to fill a need.

Israel had demanded a king before God was ready to name a king. However, what God *did* need and what Israel truly needed — as opposed to what they wanted — was someone to unite them and lead them in battle. They were about to be overrun by the pagan tribes which their ancestors had failed to deal with when they entered the land. (Deut. 7:1-4.)

God had raised up judges in the 400 years since Joshua fought the battle of Jericho in times of national danger. So this time, He raised up a warrior/leader, but to satisfy the Israelites, He anointed Saul "king."

Saul was there at a time when God had a need. (1 Sam. 9:16.) This was a special time for a special man to fill a special need.

Saul was made king primarily in order to lead Israel against the Philistines, who had captured the ark of the covenant.

The elders of Israel had foolishly demanded it be taken from the tabernacle at Shiloh and brought into battle. Instead of looking to God for help, they were making an idol out of the ark, and God allowed it to be captured. (1 Sam. 4:4-11.)

Samuel, the 15th and final judge of Israel, as well as prophet, was told by God on the day before Saul came hunting donkeys:

About this time tomorrow I will send you a man from the land of Benjamin. Anoint him *leader* over my people Israel; he will deliver my people from the hand of the Philistines. I have looked upon my people, for their cry has reached me.

— 1 Samuel 9:16

In the end, however, Saul did not fully fill the need. There was "bitter war" with the Philistines during his entire reign, and finally, God was not only sorry but grieved that He had named Saul king. (1 Sam. 15:11.)

Would you not hate to have failed so that God would grieve over having given you your position? That is true failure.

The only thing Saul could have done was repent of following his own way, of giving in to pride, and begin to heed the Word of the Lord, in strict obedience. (1 Sam. 15:22,23.)

How do you find a need in any field?

The first step is to look at your abilities, at what you can do, then analyze your immediate environment to see what is lacking. What would make the job you have now work better? What is lacking in convenience or supply?

The little story about two shoe salesmen who went to Africa years ago is a graphic illustration of how attitudes or mindsets can bring failure or success: The first salesman cabled his company to bring him home because no one there wore shoes; the second salesman sent home order after order, writing to his company in excitement: "Everybody here needs shoes!"[2]

The first salesman never explored all possibilities before giving up; the second man looked for needs that he could fill.

Also, I cannot say too often that all of the principles in this book are predicated on one's being in the will of God and obedient to His leading. Some of the men we have used as examples may not have been Christians, but the particular characteristics I have used as examples are true whether or not one is saved.

God's laws and principles are true in the natural *and* the spiritual realm. The difference is in natural and eternal goals. A Christian can take these same principles for success in life and apply them to his spiritual race. In fact, all of us ought to be doing just that.

Turn to the Contents page and read the chapter titles. They make a list of the steps needed for ministry or simply to live a Christian life in the pattern of Jesus.

The next chapter and this one may seem to overlap; however, the next chapter is about reaching out and helping other people in specific, individual cases. This chapter was about finding a generic need, a general need that will benefit many in society in general, that only you can fill at a particular time.

This chapter is about your vocation, the next one about your responsibility to other people as a Christian. You might say that this chapter is about *you*, while the next chapter is about others.

---

[1]*New Dictionary of Thoughts*, "Success," p. 645, Charles Buxton (1823-1871).

[2]*Encyclopedia of 7700 Illustrations*, p. 1565, #7119.

16

Meet the Needs of Others

One thing I know: the only ones among you who will be really happy are those who will have sought and found how to serve.[1]

– Albert Schweitzer

Meeting the needs of others means that you are doing what Jesus told His disciples to do just before the triumphal entry into Jerusalem on what we now celebrate as "Palm Sunday":

> **. . Whoever wants to become great among you must be your servant, and whoever wants to be first must be your slave — just as the Son of Man did not come to be served, but to serve, and to give his life as a ransom for many.**

> **Matthew 20:26-28**

The turning point in Saul's office as king, the point at which he began to turn off the "straight and narrow" path, was not a carnal sin of the mind and body, but a sin of the soul and spirit.

In a rash moment, "feeling his oats" as one who has power over others, he made a vow to God.

Making vows to God is serious business. Whether you know it or not, He takes you at your word, because He keeps His Word. (Eccle. 4:4-6.) It is better not to make vows unless you know for sure you can keep them. In addition, Saul's vow involved a curse on anyone else who broke it.

Saul made this vow out of his mind, not checking with the Lord, and out of pride. This is the first time we see pride rise up in Saul in the biblical account, and I believe, it marks the downturn of his tenure as king. Not only did he make this vow for his own ego, but he never thought about, or tried to meet, the needs of his people.

> **. . . Saul had bound the people under an oath, saying, "Cursed be any man who eats food before evening comes, before *I have avenged myself on my enemies!*" So none of the troops tasted food.**
>
> **1 Samuel 14:24**

When did the Philistines become Saul's personal enemies?

When did they stop being God's enemies and the people's enemies?

When did Saul become the "big I" and the people the "little you"?

The Israelite soldiers were "in distress" that day, worn out, and needing sustenance, but they were "hamstrung" by Saul's vow. His son, Jonathan, had not heard of the vow, and when they came across a wood full of honey bee hives in the trees, he ate a piece of honeycomb. When told of the vow, he immediately saw his father had "made trouble for the country." (1 Sam. 14:24-30.)

God had not called them on a fast; Saul called them to fast. There were times in later history when God did call the kings and/or the armies to fast, and then, things went well. This time, there was trouble.

The soldiers were so hungry that night that they butchered the sheep, cattle, and calves taken as spoil and ate them with the blood, which had been absolutely forbidden by God. (Deut. 12:16-23.) For the first time, Saul also presumed on the office of priest and built an altar offering sacrifices.

God refused to answer Saul, and the whole scenario was exposed. Saul compounded the problem by promising to kill the person who had broken his vow and brought God's displeasure on them. However, his men would not let Saul put Jonathan to death, for he was more well-liked, a greater warrior than his father, and wiser as well, apparently. (1 Sam. 14:36-45.)

Every great and successful person is known for the product, service, or idea he or she gave to the world. God's principle of success is "Give to get." (Luke 6:38.) The measure of blessing and rewards we receive will be in proportion to our concern for, and help given to, others.

Serving Others Is a "Boomerang"

The Australian aborigines have a weapon called a *boomerang*. Originally, it was a curved stick designed to whip around whatever it was thrown at and return to the thrower. The word has been adopted into our everyday language as meaning something you throw at others that comes back on you. The meaning has been like the proverb that if you dig a pit for others, you may fall into it yourself. (Prov. 26:27.)

However, it also has a positive meaning, according to biblical principles. Giving to others has the same effect. Whatever you do for another, you do for yourself, in a sense, because everything you do which benefits *or* injures another will come back to you.

Another aspect of the boomerang factor to take into consideration is that what comes back usually is greatly multiplied. This is simply another way of saying, "What you sow, you reap." The force with which you "threw" will be enhanced by the speed and distance involved, so that what you threw comes back to you with greater force.

In God's economy, generally speaking, one seed returns a harvest of much fruit. God is a God of multiplication, which can work for your good or your downfall. His instructions to Adam and Eve included "to multiply" themselves. (Gen. 1:28.) From one couple has resulted billions of people.

Faith in God and His opinion of us is the only means by which we may shut out of our minds the deadly effects of past experiences of suffering and unpleasantness events.

Your earthly destiny is largely a matter of the extent to which you accept the responsibility of controlling and directing your mind. If you believe in your dreams, there is no limit to what you can do.

Therefore, you may fail alone — although it is highly unlikely that anything you do will not affect other people — but certainly, you will not succeed alone. Man was created to be a family, not a race of individuals, each living in his own world. The Church is a Body, with each of us having his or her place and role.

If you do not work with the "cells" on each side of you, it not only means you fail, but it spills over into their lives. Conversely, if you succeed, it will be partly because you received help from those around you.

No one truly walks alone. All that you send forth into the lives of others will come back into your own. First Peter 4:10 in *The Living Bible* says:

God has given each of you some special abilities; be sure to use them to help each other, passing on to others God's many kinds of blessings.

A word to the wise is: Sow seeds of your own success by helping others succeed along the way. Also, if you want to be encouraged in your "down" times, encourage others. Help them to see themselves as they will be, just as you try to see yourself that way, knowing that God "is still working on you."

---

[1]Quote from Albert Schweitzer in Mom, (Chatham Publications, 1994), p. 17.

17

See Yourself as You Will Be

No amount of accomplishment can replace the power and the motivation of finding your own special niche and working toward your dreams.[1]

If Abraham had seen himself as he really was — already an old man with an old wife and no children — he would have seen a hopeless situation. However, he saw himself as God promised: father of more descendants than could be counted. (Gen. 12:1-3.)

If Saul of Tarsus had seen himself as he really was — a stubborn, opinionated Pharisee, zealous for the Mosaic law and against the followers of Christ — he never would have become the greatest writer of the New Testament. (Acts 22:3-5.) However, after the experience on the road to Damascus, he did see himself as he would be, as Jesus saw him: Paul, perhaps the greatest apostle. (Acts 9:3-9.)

If Adam and Eve could have seen themselves through God's eyes, as they would be when matured by growing in His will, the entire history of this planet would have been different. However, they had to take one step at a time, just as we do. Every step needs to be taken under the guidance of the Holy Spirit, if you are to reach your potential.

As far as outward actions were concerned, King Saul began not only to take one step at a time but to keep walking. However, what did not continue to mature was Saul's attitude about himself. Nor did he take another step and keep walking *with* God, only in his duties as king.

Each person setting out on the road to his or her goal needs to have a figurative "experience on the road to Damascus." If you are called to minister, use imagination to see yourself ministering to crowds or in churches. If you have an idea for an invention, see yourself as you will be when it is successful.

If as boys and girls, we could see ourselves as we will be in old age, most of us probably would live differently. You will never fulfill your vision if you continue to think of yourself as you are now.

Women happily expecting babies used to see themselves already as mothers. They began to think more of the baby's needs than their own. Many problems with children and young people today come from the fact that too many expectant mothers do not do this anymore. They continue to see themselves as independent with no responsibilities, so the babies become burdens.

The same thing is true with young men. When they plan to marry, they ought to see themselves as no longer single, no longer footloose and fancy-free, but part of a larger whole, moving into a greater fulfillment and happiness.

When Samuel greeted Saul, he could not grasp that the future had opened before him. He could not imagine becoming something he had never in his wildest dreams considered. The first thing he said placed him in a box of his own thinking: an insignificant member of the least significant clan of the smallest tribe.

Somehow, he never was able to get past that image of himself with any real understanding. I think that, inside, until he died he was "an insignificant member of the least significant clan of the smallest tribe in Israel," although he was on the throne.

He was a king on the outside to all intents and purposes, yet on the inside, he saw himself as a Benjamite youth who would never amount to anything. It was a tragedy for him and for his descendants that he never let God show him who he really could be. He never grew into his full potential as a human being and as king.

Let God Show You Who You Are

Get a pad and pencil and write down who you are at this point in time. In an earlier chapter, I talked about finding out who you are — not someone's son or daughter, father or mother, not identified by your work or profession. You are a child of God, first, but what does that mean specifically? Make a list of characteristics that you think fit you:

- I am kind, hardworking, good-hearted, patient . . . .

- I am trustworthy, confident (and whatever else you think about yourself).

Then make a list of what you can do:

- I can write, or sing, or paint, or type well, or even, clean houses well. People have become great successes with cleaning businesses or related enterprises.

- I can sell things or I can build things.

- I am good with people, or I am good at planning.

Put all of that together and get a picture of who you are as a child of God at this point in time. Then use your imagination to let the Holy Spirit show you what you will be.

Faith is the only means by which we may eliminate the deadly effects of past experiences of suffering and unpleasantness from our minds. Your earthly destiny is largely a matter of the extent to which you accept the responsibility of controlling and directing your mind.

Your mental attitude needs discipline and control at all times. Self-discipline would carry you through years of aching discouragement and defeat, if that were necessary to eventually reach your goal. We have talked of many people already who succeeded after years and years of trying, and even after many failures.

Without self-discipline in their thinking as well as perseverance in their actions, they would not have been able to keep on until they were successful in what they set out to do.

The psalmist wrote that our souls (mind, will, and emotions) are like minor children in that they have to be weaned from childish wants, needs, and desires and gently but firmly disciplined to continue in the right way.

But I have stilled and quieted my soul; like a weaned child with its mother, like a weaned child is my soul within me.

Psalm 131:2

We are prone to indulge in the emotions of self-pity, I-want-my-way, the someone-is-picking-on-me syndrome of blaming others, this is too hard, life is not fair, and so forth on and on. Without disciplining our thoughts by an act of will, our emotions will run wild.

It is very easy to give up, even before you start, if you allow negative thoughts to run your life. If you believe in your dreams, there is no limit to what you can do. Jesus told His disciples:

". . . I tell you the truth, if you have faith as small as a mustard seed, you can say to this mountain, 'Move

102

from here to there' and it will move. Nothing will be impossible for you."

Matthew 17:20

Faith is faith, although we usually take that verse as meaning things outside of ourselves, such as circumstances, financial problems, and so forth. However, the principle is true in all areas. Have faith in yourself and that mountain of low self-esteem, lack of self-worth, negative words spoken over you by others, and fear will have to move out of your way.

The mustard seed found in the Middle East and spoken of by Jesus in Matthew 17:20 is one of the smallest seeds of all.

. . . I tell you the truth, if you have faith as small as a mustard seed, you can say to this mountain, 'Move from here to there' and it will move. Nothing will be impossible for you.

That much faith will move that mountain from "here," your present, to "there," your past, where you can walk off and leave it behind. However, do not wait to move forward until it is behind you. No successful person ever "measured up" to his full potential when he started out.

[1]Munroe, Myles. *The Pursuit of Purpose*, (Shippensburg: Destiny Image Publishers; copyright 1992 by Myles Munroe), p. 4.

18

Don't Refuse To Start Up Just Because You Don't Yet Measure Up

In ancient days, the most celebrated precept was, "Know thyself". . . . (Samuel Johnson) It is not the situation which makes the man, but the man which makes the situation. (F.W. Robertson)[1]

Capability and *ability* come from the same root, yet they are not the same thing. "Ability" is what you are able to do now; "capability" is what you can do in the future, if you exert yourself and keep trying.

When Samuel looked for Saul in order to anoint him king, the young man had disappeared. Hiding in the baggage, as Saul did that day (1 Sam. 10:21b), showed that in his own thinking, he had neither the ability nor the capability of being king.

However, we have to give Saul credit for the fact that he did not refuse to start because he did not yet measure up to kingship in his own eyes. Spiritually, he may not ever have measured up to fill the shoes of a godly king; however, in the natural, Saul grew to fit the throne.

105

As Christians, we want to not only measure up in the natural, but in the spiritual realm. We want to "grow into the shoes" of the person God sees us as and has destined us to be. However, we can never get to be that person without beginning where we are and taking one step at a time.

Start now with what you have and where you are. Charles Goodyear, founder of the Goodyear Tire Co., began his experiments in vulcanized rubber while he was in prison. He saw the person he could and would become, and took one step at a time to get there.

John Bunyan wrote the Christian classic, *Pilgrim's Progress*, while in prison. He did not let life just happen to him, but even in terrible circumstances continued to move toward the goal God had set for him.

The quickest way to be a failure is to let life happen to you, instead of taking authority over your own destiny and beginning to move toward it.

Yes, sometimes, you do have to change your goal if you have a specific one in mind, and it becomes apparent that it is not going to work. For example, suppose the goal you set out to reach was to discover the next comet to pass close enough to earth to be seen. Then two men, Hale and Bopp, find it before you. (At least one other man discovered the comet, now known as Hale-Bopp, in 1995 and reported it only one-half hour after the other two.)

What do you do? Give up? No, you keep looking for the next one. Those two men saw themselves as discoverers of comets, when one was an amateur and the other an astronomer, but not the best nor the most well-known. If they had waited to become the best known, neither would have gone down in history among a select few successful sky watchers.

Yes, sometimes, you have to change the way you are trying to reach your goal, as those scientists do who try one experiment after another to gain the end result.

Yes, sometimes you have to change your location to be successful. You cannot see comets very well if you are using a telescope in a large city where the reflected lights hide the stars. Both Hale and Bopp were in sparsely populated desert states (New Mexico and Arizona) where city lights do not obscure the night sky.

The fact remains, however, that nothing will happen until you take that first step. How do you know what that first step is? Once you know your goal, know your abilities, and your capabilities, then learn everything you can about your vision.

Too many people remain like a scrap in the wind, blown here and there, with seemingly no control over their destinies. Longfellow wrote a poem around the refrain from a Lapland song in which he extolled the state of youth when things are "fresh and fair" and anything seems possible.

A boy's will is the wind's will, and the thoughts of youth are long thoughts.[2]

The Door to Success Is Belief

The "door" to a mindset of success is to retain that "boy's will" and the "long thoughts" of youth as the first step. Do not ever let yourself lose the freshness and the optimism of believing that anything you set yourself to do is possible with God.

However, to that thought as "direction finder" must be added the knowledge of who you will be, of where you want to go, and of how to get there. How to get there involves finding out all that you can about whatever it is you want to do. Also, find out what others have done that worked and what they did that did not work.

English statesman Edmund Burke wrote that the biggest difference between a real leader in any field and a pretender is that:

The one sees into the future, while the other regards only the present; the one lives by the day, and acts on expediency; the other acts on enduring principles and for immortality.[3]

Pretenders daydream instead of visualizing how to reach their goals.

Pretenders are moved by circumstances, not their visions.

Pretenders fool themselves, but almost never fool others.

Saul grew to become a true leader in the natural, if not in a spiritual sense. Without a vision of being king, he became truly king after he was thrust into that position. If there was pretense, it was in his standing with God. That cost his posterity the throne.

A 20-mile race begins with one step; however, one step won't take you very far if you quit there. You have to keep walking. "By the inch, it's a cinch," the tortoise told the hare in Aesop's fable. And look who won the race!

It is not how fast you make it, but *whether* you make it.

It is not whether you yet measure up to your potential, but whether you have started in that direction.

It is not who you are now, but who you will be that determines your success; however, who you will be depends on your present attitude toward, and belief in, yourself.

It is not whether you are perfect, but whether you are moving toward your goal. You cannot win the race if you do not start.

---

[1]Edwards, Tryon, Sr. Ed.; Browns, Ralph Emerson, Revision Ed. *The New Dictionary of Thoughts*, p. 312, "Inquisitiveness," Samuel Johnson (English author and lexicographer, 1709-1784); p. 386, "Man," F.W. Robertson (English minister, 1816-1853).

[2]Aldington, Richard, Ed. *The Viking Book of Poetry of the English-Speaking World*, Vol. II, p. 825; Henry Wadsworth Longfellow, "My Lost Youth."

[3]*The New Dictionary of Thoughts*, p. 638; Burke, Edmund (1729-1797), English orator and statesman.

19

Don't Quit Because
You Are Not Perfect

Some men give up their designs when they have almost reached the goal; while others, on the contrary, obtain a victory by exerting, at the last moment, more vigorous efforts than before.[1]

– Polybius

This chapter is an extension of the last chapter because:

It is just as important not to quit when you realize you are not perfect as it is to go ahead and take those first steps when you realize you do not yet measure up to your potential.

It is not enough to put one foot in front of the other and keep walking in order to measure up; it is just as imperative to keep walking if you find that, for some reason, your capabilities are not what you thought. Or perhaps it is taking you longer than you thought to get there. Or perhaps you thought you had to be perfect in order to achieve success.

There are many people who have seen themselves as they would be if they continued to reach toward their goals and have been eager to start knowing they would measure up as they grew. Yet some of those unfortunately quit along the path, because in the period of time they expected, they did not become perfect.

Others have succeeded without much trouble until, one day, they made a mistake. Then they became like Judas. They judged themselves, sentenced themselves, and figuratively "committed suicide" by giving up. They became failures because they either expected too much of themselves or thought more highly of themselves than they should have (pride).

The Apostle Paul warned against thinking too highly of ourselves, but in the same sentence he advised us to "judge" ourselves in line with the measure of faith God has given us:

> **. . . Do not think of yourself more highly than you ought, but rather think of yourself with sober judgment, in accordance with the measure of faith God has given you.**
>
> **Romans 12:3**

There is one good thing we can say for King Saul: He refused to give up. He knew he was not perfect, but he did not quit. Once he was anointed king of Israel, he never considered giving up the throne because he was not perfect. In fact, he went overboard in trying to hang onto it. Saul was not a quitter.

He had shortcomings, obviously, and he thought less of his abilities than Samuel did. Samuel grieved over his downfall until God had to speak very sternly to the prophet:

> **. . . How long will you mourn for Saul, since I have rejected him as king over Israel? Fill your horn with oil and be on your way . . . .**
>
> **1 Samuel 16:1**

Yet God allowed Saul to retain the throne for a number of years after that. Those years were spent perfecting the next king,

David, through trials and tribulations in order that he might be proved worthy of the office.

Henry Ward Beecher, famous New England minister and author in Civil War days, wrote:

> The difference between perseverance and obstinacy is, that one often comes from a strong will, and the other from a strong won't.[2]

I am afraid that in the story of the making of a king, Saul's perseverance became obstinacy in the long run. A successful person does not give up, but he has the sense to know the difference between failure and a lost cause.

Giving up in defeat is not the same as giving up on a lost cause, if and when you are sure that is the case. However, that does not mean giving up entirely. That means finding another way to go.

---

[1]*New Dictionary of Thoughts*, p. 477, "Perseverance," Polybius (205-123 B.C.), Greek historian.

[2]Ibid, p. 478, Henry Ward Beecher (1813-1887).

20

Ride Above the Waters of the Commonplace

Greatness carries with it experiences so unique that they can be shared with no one else for sheer lack of ability to communicate effectively.

As you proceed along the way to the fulfillment of your vision or dream, it will become necessary to separate yourself at times from the common or the commonplace. Samuel set Saul a pattern or example of this from the very beginning.

> **After they came down from the high place to the town, Samuel talked with Saul on the roof of his house. . . . As they were going down to the edge of the town, Samuel said to Saul, "Tell the servant to go on ahead of us ""— and the servant did so — "but you stay here awhile, so that I may give you a message from God."**
>
> **1 Samuel 9:25,27**

In order to hear from God or to learn from his counselor, Saul had to separate himself from the servant, now a "commoner," and get away from the commonplace things of everyday life. All through the Bible, you will see that men of

God drew apart from the common and the commonplace in order to stay on track or to get direction for the next step.

The first thing Jesus did after His baptism was to go apart into the wilderness for forty days of fasting, prayer, and facing temptation. (Luke 4:1-13.) Throughout His ministry, the writers of the gospels mention that He "went aside," or "went up on the mountain," or on one occasion, sent them across the Sea of Galilee ahead of Him. (Matt. 14:22,23.)

Immersing yourself all of the time in the "sea of humanity" will smother you, even if you are only wading in the "back-waters" of that sea and are not a celebrity or famous person. Some solitude is necessary not just for reaching your long-term goal, but for achieving successful steps along the way.

However, solitude will not help you unless you use it rightly. Separating yourself from the common and the commonplace must be from necessity, not from feeling yourself better than those around you. Again, motive is the key to whether this principle is positive or negative.

After he was well and truly seated on the throne, King Saul too often used his times of separation from the common and the commonplace to brood over past failures or fancied wrongs done to him by David. In fact, he slipped into the darkness of depression. (1 Sam. 16.)

These times only occurred after "the Spirit of the Lord had departed from Saul," and David had been anointed future king in his place. About the time this happened, Saul was told of David the musician, and he had the young man brought to court.

When David played the harp, the evil spirit of depression left Saul (1 Sam. 16:23), and he gained relief. Saul "brooded" because the Holy Spirit had left him; however, anyone can slip into depression if he broods over past mistakes or failures.

Saul's emotions were in a turmoil, because his will was set with himself and not with God. The early Church leader Augustine wrote:

> The important factor in those emotions is the character of a man's will. If the will is wrongly directed, the emotions will be wrong; if the will is right, the emotions will be not only blameless, but praiseworthy. The will is engaged in all of them; in fact, they are all essentially acts of will.[1]

In other words, as David wrote about his soul: "weaning" it or letting it run wild is simply a choice, an act of will. In fact, so many things in life boil down to simple choices.

Choose Against Negative Input

Learn to watch out for negative thoughts, or emotions in turmoil, in your times of solitude. Cast them down as if they were so many pesky mosquitoes buzzing around your head. Separating yourself from the commonplace, the ordinary routine, is for constructive purposes, not destructive.

Time alone is for refreshing your spirit.

Time alone is for renewing your mind.

Time alone is for resting your body and your emotions.

Time alone is for meditating on the scriptures and for hearing ideas and inspiration from the Holy Spirit.

Time alone is for developing a closer fellowship with God.

Time alone is for hearing from Jesus what your next step ought to be.

Time alone is for "taking stock" of where you are and what you have accomplished.

The noise of constant voices, no matter how interesting the dialogue and conversation, acts on your mind and spirit like pebbles splashing into a pool of quiet water. The result is no more quiet water, no more reflective pool, but turmoil. English clergyman Lawrence Sterne once wrote:

> In solitude, the mind gains strength, and learns to lean upon itself; in the world, it seeks or accepts of a few treacherous supports — the feigned compassions of one, the flattery of a second, the civilities of a third, the friendship of a fourth; they all (can) deceive . . . .[2]

Another wise man wrote that an hour of thoughtful solitude may "nerve the heart" for days of conflict — "girding up its armor to meet the most insidious foe."[3]

In addition to periodically giving yourself time to regroup, it also is imperative to surround yourself with people who are headed in the same direction, people who can add to your life and to whose lives you can contribute.

---

[1]Bettenson, Henry, translator. *Augustine's City of God*, (New York: Penguin Books, 1977, copyright by Bettenson, 1972), p. 555, Book XIV, Chapter 6.

[2]*New Dictionary of Thoughts*, p. 629, "Solitude," Lawrence Sterne (1713-1768).

[3]Ibid, James Gates Percival (1795-1856), American geologist.

21

Make Sure Those You "Flock" With Have the Right "Feathers"

Birds of a feather flock together.[1]

— Aristotle

Many "adages" and "truisms" originated in the wisdom of some of history's greatest and most successful men and women. For example, Aristotle's observation about the flocking habits of various birds applies in a figurative sense to how we choose our friends. The fact that the observation is more than 2,000 years old does not make it invalid.

I want to make a distinction, however, between seeking out the company of successful men in one's field for the gaining of more knowledge and understanding and seeking out true friends, who may not be in one's own field of endeavor. True friends are those who will "stick closer than a brother" and be there no matter what happens in your life.

So, in a sense, to succeed in reaching your goal, you may have two groups with which you "flock": those who already are successful in your field and those who have proven themselves "tried and true" and with whom God has knit your heart, as He did David and Jonathan, Saul's son. (1 Sam. 18:1.)

Ideally, some of your friends will embody both groups, because you will be like-minded and alike in heart, or "one in spirit" as were David and Jonathan. They were drawn together, and it has been my observation that both success and failure are "magnets" drawing together those of both categories.

It is almost universally true that in any meeting of salesmen, teachers, ministers, scientists, or any other such group, the crowd will divide seemingly automatically into two categories. Those who are successful or becoming so will be drawn together, and those who are not successful will find one another.

The successful associate together in the hope of picking up additional ideas; those failing seek the solace of others with whom they feel comfortable. The first group's conversation is upbeat, and the second group's conversation usually is full of defeatism: bitterness, resentment, envy, or plain old depression.

Many in the second group will be making excuses and putting down ideas and projects as unworkable, while attributing the success of the others to "luck" or favoritism. Even if I were not yet successful or in a slump, I would join the first group, because I know how to look for signs of success.

God put Saul in the right "flock" in the beginning:

> ... **Saul also went to his home in Gibeah, accompanied by valiant men** *whose hearts the Lord had touched.*
>
> **1 Samuel 10:26**

God surrounded Saul with courageous men, because his first assignment — his purpose from God — was to rid Israel of the oppression and influence of surrounding pagan tribes. The

Philistines were dominant at that time, but there also were the Ammonites, Amalekites, and others.

During his entire career as king, Saul had the company of valiant, steadfast warriors. Later, when he was under such dark depression, he sought the company of David, whose music caused the spirit of oppression to flee.

However, we do not see that Saul ever sought the company of Samuel or those prophets with whom he had prophesied in the beginning as a sovereign move of God. Samuel had to hunt for and find Saul.

The lesson we can learn from Saul's life is that it is not enough to seek out the company of those who are like-minded and successful in the field in which God has put you. As I wrote above, you also must seek out those who are like-minded in the Lord, and who believe in you and in what He has called you to do.

Pick the brains of the first group as often and as much as you possibly can and rely on the encouragement and support of the second group.

Choice of Friends Can Make or Break You

In addition, it is very helpful in difficult or important times to gather a special group of people together for prayer and counsel. However, once again make sure your counselors are people who believe in God, in His Word, and in you. You do not need "naysayers" giving you negative counsel.

Solomon, noted for his wisdom, wrote much about gathering people around you who can give good counsel. He said there was safety in a "multitude of counselors." (Prov. 11:4.) Without such counsel, purposes are defeated, Solomon wrote. (Prov. 15:22.) He also wrote that the man who "walks with wise men" will be wise. (Prov. 13:20.)

There were those available, in addition to the warriors and prophets, with whom Saul could have surrounded himself. He would have profited greatly from their counsel and support. They were of the tribe of Issachar.

Men of Issachar, who understood the times and knew what Israel should do — 200 chiefs, with all their relatives under their command.

1 Chronicles 12:30

Your choice of friends in many cases can make or break you. Look at the promising young men and women whose lives have been ruined simply because they chose friends who led them astray. Some of the best advice I have collected from wise men involves one's choice of friends.[2]

- A friend should be one whose understanding and virtue we can trust, and whose opinion we value for justness and sincerity.

- A man who makes a friend both wise and sympathetic has doubled his mental resources.

- One of the biggest blessings in life is "a prudent friend."

- True friendship gives life to a relationship; false friendship decays and ruins whatever it touches.

- Always choose friends one can look up to in some way, who can be valued not only because they like you, but because they have character and integrity.

- A true friend will not only encourage, support, and give you honest advice, but will forgive your human failings. (I did not say ignore failings, but *forgive*, not judge and condemn.)

The late author Pearl S. Buck wrote:

The person who tries to live alone will not succeed as a human being. His heart withers if it does not answer another heart. His mind shrinks away if he hears only the echoes of his own thoughts and finds no other inspiration.[3]

Another has written that, "A true friend is the gift of God, and only He who made hearts can unite them."[4]

As Christians, if we do not recognize and accept those God has "surrounded" us with and with whom He united us in heart, we have no true friends.

It is very important, however, to make a distinction between friends who tell us the truth in kindness and love and those whose words "for your own good" are critical and cynical. The words of a friend may wound one's pride, but the words of a false friend will wound one's soul and spirit.

> **Wounds from a friend can be trusted, but an enemy multiplies kisses.**
>
> **Proverbs 27:6**

> **A man's spirit sustains him in sickness, but a crushed (wounded) spirit who can bear?**
>
> **Proverbs 18:14**

Christian motivational speaker and writer Van Crouch has written that noted radio commentator Paul Harvey once gave him some good advice: "Van, if you want to get big fleas, hang out with big dogs."[5]

Critics, losers, and detractors of others are not "big dogs," but little dogs like Pekinese, whose bark is frequent and loud but avails nothing. Ignore such people.

---

[1]*New Dictionary of Thoughts*, "Familiar Phrases," p. 751, Aristotle, *Rhetoric*, I, xi, 25.

[2]Some of the quotes are my own; some are either exact or paraphrased quotes from the category of "Friendship" in *The New Dictionary of Thoughts*, pp. 223-225.

[3]Buck, Pearl S.

[4]*New Dictionary*, p. 225; Robert South (1634-1716), English theologian.

[5]Crouch, Van. *Stay in the Game*, (Tulsa: Harrison House, 1989), p. 197.

22

Ignore Detractors, Losers, and Critics

. . . Do not imagine that those who make the most noise are the only inhabitants of the field. . . .[1]

– Edmund Burke

A person who has a close relationship with the Lord will be able to discern the difference between a true friend and a false friend. However, there may be *some* truth in the words of a false friend, so it is wise to separate the words someone speaks from his motives.

Be willing to learn from any experience. True friends may be too kind to tell you faults that are hindering you. Sometimes it is wise to learn from one's critics; however, do not let hurt feelings keep you from hearing any truth involved. Unfortunately, other people may see us better than we see ourselves.

Remaining open to constructive criticism is a sign of one who is teachable. Being closed to observations that could be instructive and helpful in motivating one to change is a sign of a donkey. However, *destructive* criticism is not helpful but harmful.

Someone has said that cynical people know the price of everything but the value of nothing. This adage sums up those who try to tear down other people. Usually, this attitude is because they are failures themselves in some way and prone to project bitterness, envy, and a sense of failure onto those who are successful.

Saul's detractors were envious of a common man, who was not of the tribe of Judah or Ephraim (the two most prestigious), but of the smallest and least significant, being elevated to high position in which he would rule over them.

We see this tendency running rampant in American culture today. The successful immediately become fair game for the barbs and slighting remarks of the news media. God help those leaders who are not perfect in every way, because the media will "cut them no slack"!

Those who do fail in any way are the focus of what has come to be called "the feeding frenzy" of the reporters and photographers of various elements of the media, like sharks sensing blood and moving in for the kill. The whole quote from Edmund Burke, which I used at the opening of this chapter, is very astute:

> Because half-a-dozen grasshoppers under a fern make the field ring with their importunate chink, whilst thousands of great cattle repose beneath the shadows of the British oak, chew the cud, and are silent, pray do not imagine that those who make the noise are the only inhabitants of the field; that, of course, they are many in number; or that, after all, they are other than the little, shriveled, meager, hopping — though loud — and troublesome insects of the hour.[2]

Learn to ignore the "troublesome insects" who make the most noise. Detractors usually are very loud and vociferous.

Saul had to deal with those at the start of his kingship, as we have seen in earlier chapters.

> **There were, however, some bums and loafers who exclaimed, 'How can this man save us?' And they despised him and refused to bring him presents,** *but he took no notice.*
>
> **1 Samuel 10:27** (TLB)

We see this attitude often in business when one person is promoted over the heads of those who consider themselves more deserving or qualified.

We see this carping attitude even in churches when the leadership elevates someone in the congregation to a position of authority.

Because of this tendency of human nature, it is wise to periodically examine your friendships. Pay attention to the words, tones, and attitudes of those you have felt were your friends.

A prophecy of Jesus was that He would be wounded "in the house of his friends." (Zech. 13:6.) In fact, it seems we are more apt to be wounded by friends than by enemies.

Examine Your Friendships

I would suggest that now might be a good time to count your friends, whether they are blessings or hindrances. Think of those who are closest to you. It might even be helpful to make a list on paper. Then write down their attitudes to you, to themselves, and to life.

1. Is each of them positive in speaking of you, themselves, or others?

2. Is any of them highly critical of others, yet pats himself on the back? Are his or her comments always prefaced with, "I

did this or that," or "I always do it this way," implying that any other way is wrong?

3. Is his or her first remark on any subject one of "I-know-best" and "you-are-wrong"?

Taking a good look at those with whom you are "flocking" may help you get out of a "slough of depression," as John Bunyan called times of discouragement.[3] If you find most of your friends are like this, then it is time to take a good look at your own attitudes. Why are you hanging around negative people?

If you realize you need to change your class of friends, be careful how you do it. What you sow will come back to you. Be tactful, be gradual in moving away from them, and do not become judgmental and critical in your own turn.

Judging someone's works and/or attitudes does not mean judging the person. That is God's prerogative, not yours. (Luke 6:37.)

We need other people. God did not create man to be alone. Poet John Donne often is quoted in various contexts — some biblically right and some not — but what he said is very true:

> **No man is an *Island*, entire of it self; Every man is a piece of the *Continent*, part of the main. . . .[4]**

Daniel Webster wrote:

> Man is a special being, and if left to himself, in an isolated condition, would be one of the weakest creatures; but associated with his kind, he works wonders.[5]

There are 10 "Big Fs" — not "ifs" — you must deal with which form your focus in life through their interworking:

Facts (not just education, but how your society or culture operates), fate (or your personal circumstances), foolishness (or misjudgment), fences (various limits of mind, body, society, an so forth), force (will power), fantasy (imagination and vision), facade (the front you decide to show the world), failure or fulfilment, fear, and faith.

Do these influences cause life to be fixed, firm, and final? Some believe so. Or is life flexible, able to be fashioned and formed in spite of those ten things? I believe the latter. You can take control of the direction of your life through prayer and study and through the feedback of good friends and counselors.

Surround yourself with God as your spiritual Father, with supportive family members, pastors who are true undershepherds for the Lord, spiritual advisors, friends in your church and in organizations to which you belong. There are many social and civic organizations where you can meet people whom you can help and who can add to your life.

"Hanging out" with successful people and ignoring those who try to "cut you down" will put you in a position to broaden your own experience and knowledge.

---

[1]Burke, Edmund. From "Letter to a Member of the National Assembly (1791), *Oxford Book of Quotations*, p. 111, #16.

[2]Ibid.

[3]Bunyan, John (1628-1688). *Pilgrim's Progress*, first published in 1678.

[4]Donne, John (1571-1631). *Meditation XVII*, quote taken from *The Oxford Book of Quotations*, p. 190.

[5]*Instant Quotation Dictionary*, p. 176.

23

Broaden Your World Through Knowledge and Experience

If you know you do not know everything you need to know, but have no desire to learn more – your world is too small! If you think you already know everything you need to know – certainly your world is too small!

It may sound contradictory, but the first step to knowledge – of yourself or of the field you have chosen – is to admit ignorance. The second step is to desire to dissipate that ignorance; and, the third step is to take action to gain the knowledge you do not have.

Even if you think you already know a certain amount in your field, it would behoove you to lay it aside and begin at "square one." Admit ignorance either literally or voluntarily, then you have nowhere to go but up.

Concerning your ownself, say to the Lord: "I do not know yet what kind of person I am going to be. Please show me."

Concerning your goal, admit to yourself, "I do not know everything I need to know about this," and ask the Holy Spirit to give your guidance.

Concerning the field in which you are now working, even if it is not your ultimate goal, ask the Lord to help you learn more about this field and to improve your skills and abilities.

Then expect to begin to receive understanding about yourself, about your present abilities, and more importantly, about your capabilities. Your part is to look for books, publications, or even night courses to improve your knowledge.

I have found that most people are capable of doing nearly anything to which they put their minds and hands wholeheartedly. (The only place *success* comes before *work* is in the dictionary.) However, there is no substitute for knowing everything there is to know about what you want to do.

Work will not substitute for knowledge, but neither will knowledge substitute for work. Knowing something and acting on it will bring results, and result by result, you will gain success.

Lord Francis Bacon said that knowledge is power, yet others with perhaps more understanding, have said:

> ... Mere knowledge is not power; it is only possibility. Action is power; and its highest manifestation is when it is directed by knowledge. (T.W. Palmer) Knowledge . . . is power in the sense that wood is fuel. Wood on fire is fuel. Knowledge on fire (in action) is power. (H. Mackenzie)[1]

When God gives you a vision or has assigned you something to do, it is to your advantage to get every bit of information possible about it. Do research in the area of your vision, write it down, and make it plain. (Hab. 2:2.) Any enterprise constructed on wise planning becomes strong through commonsense. (Prov. 24:3,4.)

In the world, understanding your product or your type of service is essential for success. The same thing is true in the spiritual realm. No one has a "corner" on the market of ideas and knowledge.

Ask the Holy Spirit to develop your understanding. Knowledge plus understanding equals wisdom.

Two teachers saw a need and set themselves the goal of establishing a lending library. They were successful from the "get-go." Why? They quickly achieved success by taking the right first step: finding out everything they could about what they wanted to do.

They studied other libraries. They compiled all the information they could about that business — suppliers, equipment, buildings, methods, and advertising to attract customers. I am sure anyone who has a successful business of any kind has done the same thing.

You can obtain all the knowledge you need from observation, experimentation, studying and reading, talking to people in the same field, and even by employing experts or counselors who can give you good advice. My advice to anyone who wants to be successful is to develop a wide range of knowledge.

Someone has said that knowledge must be experienced to become truly known.

Knowledge Becomes Wisdom Through Experience

Saul gained knowledge by experience, which is not to be sneered at. In some fields or for some goals, experience — trial and error — is the only way to learn. However, unless you are on new and untried ground, you can learn from those who have walked the same way before you.

It is sad but true that experience cannot be transmitted from one person to another as can knowledge. You can pass on lessons you have learned from an experience as objective information, but the actual experience is subjective and only yours.

It was not necessary for Saul to actually take Jericho as Joshua did in order to learn warfare. However, Joshua was starting out in untried territory with no experience in leading armies into battle. Nevertheless, Joshua had knowledge of how to fight before he began. Where did he get it? From Jesus Himself, most Bible scholars believe. (Josh. 5:13-6:5.)

The point is: Get knowledge from wherever and however you can, and as Solomon wrote, "with all your knowledge, get understanding." (Prov. 2:2.)

Samuel led Saul to *broaden his world by developing a wide range of associations.* This knowledge stood him in good stead as he began to experience actually being king. This principle is not stated specifically in any one place in Saul's story; however, by looking at what Samuel did, you can see this.

The prophet first exposed the young man to sitting at the "top table" as special guest among 30 honored guests. Saul gained knowledge of how to act when in a place of honor, which he was to experience for years to come. (1 Sam. 9:22-24.)

Samuel then had the prospective king join a band of prophets. This probably was an attempt to give him knowledge and understanding of how God directed men in that day, of what it was like to experience such an anointing, and of how it is necessary sometimes as a leader to be willing to look foolish. (1 Sam. 10:1-12.)

Thirdly, Samuel called a meeting of tribal leaders to meet and participate in crowning Saul. (1 Sam. 10:20.) Not only was this a ceremony of spiritual and national significance, but it served to introduce to Saul the vision of who he would be.

The importance of knowledge is much more noticeable in Saul's life by its absence than by its presence. Instead of focusing on learning, Saul's mind became obsessed by hate for and jealousy of David. He spent a major part of the last years of his life trying to kill the one he thought would succeed him.

As a consequence, virtually no great cultural achievements are recorded as having occurred during his reign. Compare with Saul's reign the pursuit of knowledge, culture, commerce, and spiritual matters that took place in David's and Solomon's time.

If you gain knowledge and, through experience, have gained wisdom, you have the pattern of success. This theme is stated beautifully in Ecclesiastes 7:12b (KJV):

> **. . . The excellency of knowledge is that wisdom giveth life to them that have it.**

There are two kinds of people who are bores: Those who know nothing, and those who know nothing but their own affairs or their own specialized field.

> Few men are more to be shunned than those who have time, but know not how to improve it, and so spend it in wasting the time of their neighbors, talking forever though they have nothing to say.[2]

Saul must have been terribly boring when he could talk of nothing but his own feelings and fears and his obsession with eliminating his successor. He abused the privileges of his position and missed some of the responsibilities of it.

---

[1]*New Dictionary of Thoughts*, p. 332, "Knowledge," Francis Bacon, scientist, author, and philosopher (1561-1626); Thomas Palmer, minister, (1624-1666); Henry MacKenzie (1745-1831), Scottish novelist.

[2]*The New Dictionary*, p. 67, "Bores," Tryon Edwards.

24

Understand Responsibilities as Well as Privileges

The most important thought I ever had was that of my individual responsibility to God.

– Daniel Webster

King Saul understood his responsibility as leader of Israel's armies. He fulfilled that as long as he lived. In fact, he died in battle. We can learn from his life that once we are set on an ultimate goal, we must "put our hands to the plow" and not look back.

We never see where Saul ever deviated from his responsibilities as commander-in-chief, or where he ever complained about those responsibilities and tried to get out of them. Also, he was very courageous most of the time.

Saul went to battle when he and his son Jonathan were the only ones with swords. The rest of the army only had farm implements, such as axes. The Philistines had taken all the blacksmiths out of Israel in order that swords and spears could not be made. (1 Sam. 13:19-22.) As they conquered the pagan tribes, the Israelites took swords from them.

After Saul had assumed rule over Israel, he fought against their enemies on every side: Moab, the Ammonites, Edom, the kings of Zobah, and the Philistines. Wherever he turned, he inflicted punishment on them. He fought valiantly and defeated the Amalekites, delivering Israel from the hands of those who had plundered them.

1 Samuel 14:47,48

However, apparently he never understood his responsibility to God, in spite of Samuel's tutelage. His knowledge of running with the prophets never translated into understanding. Therefore, knowledge never became experience.

His responsibility to God was simple: obedience in all things, not just in leading the army. We also can see that, even in carrying out that responsibility, he moved into self-will and insisted on doing some things his own way. (1 Sam. 13:8-14, 14:24-45, 15:1-34.) That caused him to renege or fall down in his responsibility to God.

Then the word of the Lord came to Samuel: I am grieved that I made Saul king, because he has turned away from me and has not carried out my instructions.

1 Samuel 15:10

The evening that word came to Samuel, he prayed all night for Saul, then went out the next morning to meet the king only to find that, once again, he had disobeyed God. Saul's privileges as king had "gone to his head," as we would say today. He had erected a monument in his own honor, not God's, and continued on to another place. (1 Sam. 15:12.)

There he added insult to injury by lying to the prophet (and God) and then blaming his sins on the people. (1 Sam. 15:13-21.) That is pretty typical of those who let high privilege "puff" them up and cause them to forget the responsibilities that go with position. They tend to shift blame from themselves to others. Also, they tend to want others to work for them.

Never Get "Too Good" To Work

An old story from Revolutionary War days tells of an officer who assigned some men to cut down trees to make a much-needed bridge. There were too few men to get the work done as fast as it was needed to move the troops.

Another man rode up and asked the officer in charge why he did not lend a hand himself as there was not enough help.

The officer replied in a highly indignant tone that he was a corporal! In his eyes, an officer of his rank had privilege but no responsibility to work. The passerby proceeded to dismount and pitched in to help the men until the job was done.

Then General George Washington remounted and said to the corporal as he rode off, "The next time you have a rush job and too few men, send for the Commander-in-chief, and I will come again and help."[1]

Our greatest presidents have been those who understood the relationship between responsibility and privilege. One key principle that will help you avoid this trap is: Do not ask someone else, even employees, to do something that you would not do yourself.

I have never seen or read of a truly successful person who placed privilege over responsibility. Oh, there are some famous people who do, but not great people.

We can look at the "privileges" that go with being chief executive officer of some multi-national company and envy the large salaries, fine cars and clothes, and the luxurious lifestyle. However, until you have spent one day with someone in such a position, you cannot understand the tremendous responsibilities that go with the office.

The more you rely on your "privileges," the more you will come to expect other people to do things for you and to look after you. The more you see and shoulder your responsibilities, the more you will stand on your own feet.

[1]Bennett, William J. *The Moral Compass*, (New York: Simon & Schuster, 1995), "Man Enough for the Job," retold by Ella Lyman Cabot, p. 657.

25

Stand on Your Own Feet Whenever Possible

A man of words and not of deeds is like a garden full of weeds; a man who makes full use of the hours is like a garden full of flowers.

– Anonymous

After Samuel had given Saul the various signs from God that would be fulfilled on his way home from the donkey hunt, he said:

Once these signs are fulfilled, do whatever your hand finds to do, for God is with you.

1 Samuel 10:7

In essence, the prophet advised the king-to-be that from then on, he should do whatever seemed best under the circumstances, for the Lord would guide him. At this point, even before he was openly chosen as king, the responsibility of leadership was passed on to Saul.

In most cases, this is the period in the development of a male human being that "divides the men from the boys." As long as a person has no responsibility, he will remain a perennial

"Peter Pan," someone who refuses or is unable to grow up. Responsibility brings maturity.

One of the best times in a person's life is to come to a place where he must stand on his own feet. Saul did very well in the early days, as we have seen, in doing what his hand found to do. The problem was that he went overboard, often standing on his own feet when he should have been "standing" on God.

Nevertheless, we can learn a great lesson in seeing how self-reliant Saul was in the natural.

The spirit of self-help is the root of all genuine growth in the individual; and, exhibited in the lives of many, it constitutes the true source of national vigor and strength. Help from without is often enfeebling in its effects, but help from within invariably invigorates.[1]

Ralph Waldo Emerson once said the best "lightning rod" a man can have for his protection from storms is his own backbone. The New Testament has a lot to say about "standing" for one reason or another. One who stands is not sitting or lying down or being carried by someone else.

There are times, of course, when anyone needs and must ask for and/or receive help. A successful person has no problem with either asking for or receiving help, as I talked about in an earlier chapter. However, he does not ask for help for anything he can do for himself.

A "king in the making" leads the way in doing what ought to be done. As he matures, he does what his hand finds to do, counting on God to guide him aright.

A "king in the making" does not wait for someone else to lead the fight against the enemy, nor does he find his way into the rear to be protected by the rank and file. The Bible tells us that is one reason Saul's successor, David, fell into sin **in the spring, at the time when kings go out to war** (2 Sam. 11:1).

David remained in Jerusalem that spring at loose ends, apparently restless with nothing much to do. One evening, he went up on the rooftop for some fresh air and saw the beautiful wife of a neighbor and valiant soldier in his army bathing on an adjacent roof.

This exercising of privilege and discarding of responsibility led to adultery and then to murder. Instead of standing on his own feet that year, David let his generals and subjects fight for him and got into trouble.

Perhaps not standing on your own feet will not cause you to slip into sin; however, I promise you that in some way it will cost you. If nothing else, it will offend your integrity and lower your self-esteem.

To paraphrase the earlier quote about a cynic knowing the *price* of everything but the *value* of nothing, it would seem that the *value* of anything to a person depends on the *price* he is willing to pay for it.

Some people in this country literally do have to depend on welfare to live. However, look at those who draw from the government when they could work. Many lose their self-respect, become lazy, and learn to get money by living off others, either through crimes of theft or ways that break other laws.

Benjamin Franklin, one of this country's wisest founders, coined the off-quoted saying: God helps those who help themselves, which seems to be very true.

One way to ensure that you are not hindered in carrying out responsibilities is to clear the debris out of your life.

---

[1]*The New Dictionary*, "Self-Reliance," p. 604; Samuel Smile (1812-1904), English biographer.

26

Clear Out Debris and Excess Baggage

The three traits of being able to organize, to have visions and set goals, and to persevere until goals are reached have been found more often in the lives of great achievers than high intelligence, advanced formal education, or a lot of experience in their fields.[1]

The next principle I see in Saul's life is to unclutter your life of needless and endless details and encumbrances. In 1 Samuel 10:22,23, once again we look at Saul hiding in the baggage when he should have been standing up to receive the kingship.

I use this image of "hiding behind the baggage" figuratively to embody the plight of a leader who is unable to perform his real duties because of the endless "nit-picking nothings" that tend to consume our days. Unfortunately, most of this "baggage" is not deliberately brought in — although all of us may be guilty of indulging in some "make-work" from time to time.

Once I read of an author who honestly talked of how difficult it was sometimes to get down to real creative work, spending time instead in straightening the office, sharpening pencils, and hunting exactly the right paper. (This was in the days of the typewriter.) Perhaps all of us have a few times like this when we dread starting a new project, and so forth.

However, the "mountain of baggage" of which I am thinking is made up of the details of modern living. Sometimes I wonder about how much help modern technology really is. A recent newscast said that 80 percent of the time people call somewhere on the phone, they do not get people but some kind of answering mechanism.

We can get from "here to there" much faster than our grandparents did, yet we spend much more time on the road or in the air than they did traveling by horse and buggy.

We have an untold number of "labor-saving devices" available, yet we spend more time in labor. True, we are doing more things, but we have as little or less spare time than our ancestors did.

So how can we clean some of this debris or baggage out of our lives?

Even hundreds of years before Saul, Moses found himself mired down in this problem. He literally was spending all his waking hours dealing with "piddling" little complaints and problems of the thousands of Israelites he was leading across the desert.

Today, we call those Christians who must run to the church leaders with every little problem or circumstance "high-maintenance" Christians. That means baby or teenage Christians. Moses had an entire nation of such people, most of whom seemingly were "high-maintenance" Israelites.

His father-in-law, Jethro, came for a visit and was appalled at what Moses was trying to do. He was so caught up in dealing with penny-ante complaints that he had no energy or time to be a real leader. Jethro came up with the first rule of a successful businessman, leader, or pastor: *Delegate.*

> **The next day Moses took his seat to serve as judge for the people, and they stood around him from morning till evening. . . . Moses' father-in-law replied, "What you are doing is not good. You and these people who come to you will only wear yourselves out. The work is too heavy for you; you cannot handle it alone. Listen now to me and I will give you some advice . . . .**
>
> **Exodus 18:13-19**

Jethro's advice was for Moses to choose "capable" men to take care of the lesser details of governing, leaving him free to be the "people's representative before God." (Ex. 18:19.)

Then we skip ahead in the Bible to the days of the Early Church and find the apostles in the same predicament. How did they clear out the debris of details? The same way Moses had: They delegated everyday matters to seven "deacons," in order for the apostles to have more time to pray and minister the Word of God to the people. (Acts 6:1-6.)

How To Put Your "Baggage" in Order

"Hiding behind the baggage" as Saul did will keep you from coming into your full position. In addition to delegating whatever matters you do not have to personally deal with, there are other things that can be done to clean the debris out of your working day.

There are ways to organize and make your "baggage" orderly enough so that you do not have to hide behind it. After you have delegated everything that is not absolutely your responsibility to do, then look at what is left to do in your day and set priorities.

Motivational speaker/writer Van Crouch says:

There may be successful businessmen whose desks are cluttered and who do not keep detailed lists or files. However, you will find that those men usually have things organized in their heads. They know where everything is in the midst of seeming clutter.[2]

Crouch also wrote that organization does not begin with what you do, but with the kind of person you are. Perhaps you are not naturally an organized person. If you want to fully achieve your potential and reach the goal you have set (fulfill your vision), then you will have to learn how to become organized.

The simplest way to start is to take a few minutes each morning and list what needs to be done that day. Then list these things by priorities or by necessity. You may have an appointment that is not a priority to you, but it is a necessity because you have committed to the other person to see them or to do something for them.

Look at that list carefully to see if some of it can be eliminated. Can some baggage be tossed out without causing real problems? If so, then throw it away. Look at each item to see if *you* really need to do it, or if it really needs to be done. Then delegate or eliminate.

If your desk or office is cluttered, sort the material and throw away anything no longer of use or pertinent. Have things filed by category so they are easy to find. However, do not confuse orderliness with neatness. Everything in one's office or life can be as neat as a pin, but still disorganized.

Do the same thing with your life: organize, delegate, or eliminate. Do not allow people to take up your time unnecessarily. Spend time on priorities in your own life and, then, you will have quality time and energy to contribute to other people's lives.

Is procrastination a vice of which you are guilty? Make choices not to put off until tomorrow anything you can do today. Things on which you have procrastinated should go on your list in order or priority to be eliminated one by one. Procrastination really is a thief of time.

Spanish author de Cervantes wrote that one arrives at the house of Never by traveling the street called By-and-By,[3] or as our neighbors to the South put it, "Mañana! Let's do it tomorrow."

Unsuccessful people never do today what they can put off until tomorrow. Are you one of those? It is not too late to change. Tomorrow is the first day of the rest of your life. Make it a different kind of day.

This way of dealing with the overwhelming details that come with responsibility does not mean you are not standing on your own feet. You are doing what only you can do and not doing what someone else can do in your place.

Remember that organization cannot take the place of the right attitudes, the good motivations, or the setting of visions and goals. Organization simply helps you walk efficiently along the path and in the direction those other things have set for you.[4]

In this chapter, I have discussed how not to do something: waste time. In the next chapter, I want to talk about the positive aspect of how to do something: learn the value of time and how to use it wisely.

---

[1]Synthesized from *How To Be a 10 in Business*, by Don Beveridge and Jeffrey P. Davidson, (Homewood, IL: Dow Jones-Irwin. Copyright 1988 by Beveridge and Davidson.)

[2]Crouch, pp. 109,110.

[3]*The New Dictionary*, p. 520.

[4]Crouch, p. 111.

27
Respect Time and Learn Timing

Time wasted is existence; time used is life.
Time is best killed by working it to death.
Time is the only "bank account" most of us are
*   born with. Yesterday is a canceled check,*
Tomorrow is a promissory note. Today is the only
*   "cash" you have.*

If you read the first book of the Bible, you can see that time was created along with the earth's first day. (Gen. 1:3-5.) Most people never realize the value of time until one day they wake up and realize they have spent their entire "bank account" and are bankrupt.

Somehow on some level, we do realize how valuable time is, because in the business world, it is said no telling how many times a day that "time is money." In other words, time is valuable because it makes money when wisely used and loses money when wasted.

The first night Saul stayed at the prophet's house, he slept where guests usually did in the Middle East at that time — on the roof. Sometimes there was a little room built on the usually flat roofs, such as the Shunammite woman did for the prophet

Elisha. (2 Kings 4:10.) However, most of the time, bed rolls or pads were spread on the roof itself.

At daybreak the next morning, Samuel woke Saul up, calling up to him on the roof: **. . . Get ready, and I will send you on your way** (1 Sam. 9:26).

Samuel wasted no time. Apparently everything he did for God was done efficiently, making good use of time; and, what is more, he did everything *in God's timing*, not in his own. A successful person, one who reaches goals, must understand the value of time and the value of timing.

Saul got ahead of God at least twice, when he got tired of waiting for Samuel—who was operating in God's timing—and went ahead with sacrifices which he was not authorized to offer. (1 Sam. 13:9, 15:9.)

In the last chapter, you received some ideas about how to clear the decks of debris and how to streamline your life in order to make the best use of the time you have. This is a lesson all leaders must learn in order to make progress. Slothful people spend time prodigally, as the wayward son wasted his inheritance in the parable told by Jesus. (Luke 15:11-31.)

I believe every Christian is not only to be a good steward over his resources and money, but also over his time. When you stand before the Almighty Father as Judge (Rev. 20:11-15), will you be able to give a good account of your time? If not, it is time to repent and change your thinking, as well as your use of time.

Think of Time as Money

I find it is very helpful to continue to think of time as money.

You have a bank, and its name is "Time." Every morning it credits you with 86,400 seconds. Every night it rules off—as lost—whatever of this you have failed to invest to good purpose. It carries no balances. It allows no balances. It allows no overdrafts. Each day it opens a new account for you; and each night, it burns the records of the day. If you fail to use the day's deposit, the loss is yours.[1]

Part of learning how to organize includes organizing your time, putting every minute of your day to the best use. Some of the most well-known discoveries or inventions were not the product of hours and hours of research, but were developed in someone's leisure or spare time. Those inventors made the best use of their time.

Much may be done in those little shreds and patches of time, which every day produces, and which most men throw away, but which nevertheless will make at the end of the day no small deduction from the life of a man.[2]

Some of those who used their "spare" time to good use include:

- Thomas Edison—who used his layovers as a newsboy on trains to study in town libraries, when most young people would have looked for fun or entertainment. Many of the books he studied in those times gave him knowledge or ideas for his later inventions.

- A farmer — who invented the typewriter in his spare time — and a carpenter (Eli Whitney) — who did the same with the cotton gin.

- A coal miner — who invented the locomotive — and a school teacher—who developed the telephone during after-school hours.

- Robert Fulton — who invented the steamboat — and Samuel Morse — who invented the telegraph, both in their spare time.

- John Bunyan — whom I mentioned earlier, wrote probably the greatest story of the Christian life outside the Bible while in jail for preaching. It would have been easy to waste the time by moping and feeling sorry for himself.

- Benjamin Franklin — who may have used his time better than any other inventor or scientist. No matter what he was doing as a printer and later as ambassador to foreign courts, he redeemed the time spent waiting by continuing his experiments. Franklin wrote:

If time be of all things the most precious, wasting time must be the greatest prodigality, since lost time is never found again.[3]

Even the Apostle Paul wrote his epistles while traveling, preaching, and spending time in jail. As a matter of fact, Paul wrote about the wise use of time in Ephesians 5:15,16:

Be very careful, then, how you live — not as unwise but as wise, making the most of every opportunity, because the days are evil.

The *King James Version* puts it this way:

See then that ye walk circumspectly, not as fools, but as wise, Redeeming the time, because the days are evil.

You can see that, in both versions, Paul made four points:

1. Time is valuable.

2. Misusing time is foolish, the way of fools.

3. Time is opportunity.

4. Time can be "redeemed" through good use.

Proper Timing Also Makes a Difference

Most of today's television viewers are aware that the thing which makes comedians successful or not is more than the material they have. It is *the timing* with which they deliver the "punch lines."

Timing is no less important in leadership positions or, for that matter, in your personal life. Obviously Jesus had a sense of time passing and of the scheduling of events at the proper time.

First he said, "My time has not yet come" (John 7:6); then, He said, "My time has now come" (Matt. 26:18), among other verses in which He referred to specific "times," in the sense of timing of events.

It is as unproductive to do things too soon as to do them too late. A good sense of timing is only gained in two ways: through experience and through guidance from the Holy Spirit. The man who walks in both those ways will win great victories.

The author of Ecclesiastes knew about timing:

There is a time for everything, and a season for every activity under heaven: a time to be born and a time to die, a time to plant and a time to uproot, a time to kill and a time to heal, a time to tear down and a time to build . . . .

Ecclesiastes 3:1-3

The next five verses continue to list the various things for which timing is important. The timing for planting in the western hemisphere is only in the spring, although time exists as well in the fall. Wrong timing will kill your harvest. The same is true of your business, your ministry, or your personal affairs.

If time is opportunity, we also should take a look at how problems may be turned into opportunities instead of "time-killers."

---

[1]*The Encyclopedia of 7700 Illustrations*, p. 1484, #6714, Lee, Robert G.

[2]*The New Dictionary of Thoughts*, p. 673; "Time," Caleb C. Colton (1780-1832), an English clergyman.

[3]Ibid, p. 672, Benjamin Franklin (1706-1790), American statesman, inventor, and author.

28
View Problems as Opportunities and Springboards

The things that haven't been done before
Are the tasks worthwhile today:
Are you one of the flock that follows, or
Are you one that shall lead the way?[1]

– Edgar A. Guest

Once Saul had been made king, he showed initiative and leadership by quickly grasping opportunities. Problems seemed to spur him to action — at least problems that involved action, not ones that necessitated seeking the Lord for wisdom. Again, we can learn from Saul's strong points *and* from his weak points.

Saul would not have found Samuel except for the problem of losing the donkeys and being defeated, hungry, and lost, having covered all of the territory with which he was familiar. God was leading him to Samuel and used Saul's servant to point him in the right direction.

However, Saul never saw that he needed to rely on God for direction. In terms of leading Israel against the enemy, Saul had plenty of courage. This was something he understood. You might say warfare was "known territory" to Saul, although he apparently had no experience until his first battle.

To gain victory in life, to reach the goal you believe God has set before you, to fulfill your vision, first you must have courage to deal with problems in territory known to you. However, if you progress any farther toward success, you must move out of known territory and into the unfamiliar.

At that point, you need advice from others, as we talked about in an earlier chapter, and most of all, you need guidance from the Lord. All of us from time to time figuratively come out of the known paths and reach a crossroad.

Which way do we go now? There are roads to the right and roads to the left and roads that seem straight ahead. It is possible, however — and many times, true — that the road straight ahead is not as straight and easy as it looks.

Many times the road straight ahead that seems so plainly the right way comes to a dead end, or winds up in a jungle of bushes and brambles or a field filled with weeds. In other words, it does not go anywhere.

On the other hand, so may one of the other roads. The best advice when you come to a place like that is to stand still and wait for wisdom from God. Wait for someone or something that will point you in the direction you know in your heart is right.

The late famous American poet, Robert Frost, wrote a well-known poem about this kind of quandary, about choices made concerning which road to take through life:

> I shall be telling this with a sigh
> Somewhere ages and ages hence:
> Two roads diverged in a wood, and I —
> I took the one less traveled by,
> And that has made all the difference.[2]

Frost was writing about someone choosing a road that looked more pleasant because not many people were traveling on it. Somehow that road led nowhere, and the man had great regrets at the end of his life.

This kind of road does not always "lead nowhere," however. Sometimes the "less-traveled" road is the one to take, the one that offers opportunities and challenges that most people shy away from, like a spirited horse at his shadow.

When Moses fled to the wilderness, he set foot on a 40-year path that looked as if it led nowhere. In Moses' case, the "long way around was the shortest way home," and that is sometimes the way it is. Someone has said that the "road less traveled" may be that way for a good reason!

The point is that you need the wisdom of the Lord to know which road is right for you and for His plans. How can you know which road leads to "the prophet" and kingship, so to speak, and which leads back home in defeat? For example, the donkeys had already been found. If Saul had not listened to his servant and headed back home, the whole trip would have been in vain.

The way you know which path is the right one for you — the less-traveled road or the much-traveled road — is to seek the Lord in prayer until you have a clear witness, an assurance in your heart, of which way to go.

Which brings up another point: Saul thought he was hunting donkeys, but God knew he was hunting his destiny. Are you on a search for one thing when God really is leading you to find another?

Learning To Recognize Opportunity

International teacher/evangelist Myles Munroe says that perhaps the greatest tragedy that can happen to someone is for him not to recognize his life's purpose.

No amount of accomplishments can replace the power and the motivation of finding your own special niche and working toward your dreams.[3]

Without a clear purpose, Munroe says, life becomes trial and error, a game ruled by the circumstances of one's culture and the national economy.

Saul apparently had no idea of the purpose for his life when he went hunting lost donkeys. However, the problem of not finding them was the big opportunity of his life. Someone has said opportunity can be seen easier going away from you than coming toward you, and that is very true.

Ten of the 12 men sent by Moses to "spy out" the Promised Land came back having seen nothing but problems. (Num. 13:31-33.) Joshua and Caleb saw nothing but opportunity. The ten men said everyone in that country were "giants," making them look "as grasshoppers" in their own sight.

Joshua and Caleb saw themselves and the Israelites as giants, because God had promised them the land, and with His help they would be successful. (Num. 13:30.) People with "grasshopper mentalities" will never seize available opportunities. Their "promised" lands will be lost, and they may never understand why they "die" in the wilderness of unfulfilled dreams.

Learn to look behind every problem, every challenge, that comes up in your life to see what kind of opportunity is hidden there. All opportunities do not walk up to your front door and knock. More often than not, opportunities do not wear signs lettered, "Here I am."

In fact, often a man must make his opportunities, and the best way to do that is to never accept the words "never" or "can't be done." Nearly all modern inventions were developed or discovered after a number of people had said they could not be done. Yet someone saw possibilities instead of impossibilities and did what could not be done.

During World War II, President Franklin D. Roosevelt called shipbuilder Henry Kaiser into his office to talk over a "problem," and a major problem it was. We were losing the war, because ships could not be turned out fast enough. Kaiser said he would find a way to speed up the process, which the President had been told "could not be done."

Kaiser did speed up the process with a welding process that allowed the ships to hold together as they were moved and then be turned right-side-up after assembly. The "secret" of this weld came to an entrepreneur/industrialist friend of Kaiser's, R. G. LeTourneau (a legend in his own right) in prayer, and he passed it on to Henry Kaiser.[4]

That is the way the Liberty and Victory ships began to roll off the assembly line and hasten the Allied victory in World War II. Ideas cause things to happen.

A problem became an opportunity. A challenge was accepted and answered through an idea from God. Prayer and trusting God will turn all your problems into opportunities — even if it is only the chance to build character, or develop patience, or test your abilities.

People who see and make use of opportunities are those who have taken charge of their own lives. Almost without exception, those men and women we consider great not only display leadership, but also display compassion toward their fellow men and women.

Being in control of their own lives usually gives them a better understanding of what other people are going through in their stages of growth and maturity.

Of course, not every successful person has a good heart, but the kind of successful person I am describing in this book will have concern for others. Otherwise, in my view, they really are not successful, no matter how much money, prestige, or possessions they have.

[1]Bennett, J. William. *The Book of Virtues*, (New York: Simon & Schuster, 1993), p. 488; from the poem, "The Things That Haven't Been Done Before."

[2]Robert Frost; "The Road Not Taken," *The Random House Treasury of Best-Loved Poems*, ed. Louis Phillips, (New York: Random House, Inc., 1995, 2nd. Ed.), p. 179.

[3]Munroe, Myles. *Pursuit of Purpose*, (Shippensburg, PA: Destiny Image Publishers, Inc., 1992), p. 4.

[4]Reid, Tommy. *Ethics, Excellence, and Economics*, (Tulsa: Honor Books, a division of Harrison House, 1989), pp. 158,159.

29

Move From Animal Reactions to Human Thinking

Many people talk about how we should be "fully human"; and they link that concept to the right to choose and to decision-making . . . I agree. That truth is at the heart of the scriptures. That potential is at the core of Creation.[1]

– Jimmy Reader

Modern Christians never cease to be amazed at what we would call "the lack of the milk of human kindness" exhibited by God's ancient people as recorded in the Old Testament. Society seemed to operate more in a "dog-eat-dog" standard than one of loving your brother as yourself.

For example, when Saul saved the city of Jabesh-Gilead (1 Sam. 11:12), the first thing the people did was to say without hesitation, "Bring those men here who said Saul should not be king, and we will kill them!"

But Saul said, "No one shall be put to death today, for this day the Lord has rescued Israel."

1 Samuel 11:13

161

That was one of the bright and hopeful moments in Saul's life and in Israel's history. A leader moved one step from the animal to the human. We could say that Saul "took one giant step for mankind" that day.

One of the major and beautiful themes running through the Bible is the step-by-step elevation of man's moral insights. By patient and long-suffering instructions, God developed mankind's consciences through His chosen leaders.

From the pre-flood days — when apparently there was no righteousness or morality left on earth except for Noah and his family (Gen. 6:8-10) — to the Sermon on the Mount (Matt. 5-7), there was a slow but sure increase in man's moral insights. In the New Testament, Jesus and the apostles continued to contrast the exact "eye for an eye" vengeance of the ancients to Jesus' teachings of love and forbearance.

The phrase, "Yet I show you a better way," is repeated in various contexts, stressing that love and compassion for your brothers is not only the better way, but God's way. In a rare good moment of magnanimity, Saul declined to exercise for vengeance the power available to him as king. Instead, he chose the better way of forgiveness.

What are animal reactions? These are those things people automatically do *without thinking* whether or not it is the "right" way to act. It includes unkindness to others, getting even, always pushing to get one's own way, defensiveness, indulging in all the bodily desires without listening to one's conscience, a lack of compassion, and so forth.

Man is born in his natural state with a hard heart, one that must be "circumcised" through the new birth before he can become truly "human." (Rom. 8:29.) Adam and Eve were the first humans and the only ones to be *truly human* — as defined by God's creation standard — until Jesus was born into the earth.

When the first couple "died" the day they rebelled and sinned against the Creator (Gen. 2:16,17, 3:1-14), the life of God withdrew from their hearts. This left them hardened against Him and, by extension, against one another.

Jesus admonished His disciples several times about their "hardness of heart" (Matt. 6:52; Mark 8:17-21), and probably, they were less hardened than most others in their society. The disciples had seen many signs and wonders in Jesus' ministry at that point in time, yet that knowledge and the facts of what they had seen did not change their attitudes. They still were surprised and astonished at every miracle.

They never truly understood Jesus' teachings, nor did they have faith, until they became born again (John 20:22) and received "human" hearts. Then they could believe in supernatural (spiritual) things and wait in faith for the Holy Spirit. On the day of Pentecost, they received power through the Spirit to act in faith and do the "greater works" Jesus had promised. (John 14:12.)

Those with human hearts can engage in human thinking.

Those with human hearts can interact with God, the Holy Spirit, and receive inspiration, hope, and ideas, as well as divine direction.

Those with human hearts already have entered into eternity with the Godhead and God's people, while those with Adamic, or animal hearts remain in an eternity without God.

Animal Reactions Hinder Faith

Contrary to Darwinism, man did not evolve from animal ancestors. However, the hardness of heart of people without God causes them to act more like animals than human beings in many instances. When someone excuses his immoral or unethical actions by saying, "After all, I'm only human," the truth is that he is not acting "only human," but acting as "only animal."

Many people welcomed the idea of man's evolving from animals, because it gave them an excuse to act like animals and call such behavior "only human." Another aspect of one's reactions being "animal" rather than human is that a hardened heart is more comfortable in the natural realm than in the spiritual.

"Animal reaction" does not mean simply indulging in carnal sins or "un-Christian" behavior. It means operating in a mindset that cannot believe God's promises, but can only believe what can be experienced with the five senses.

Like the disciples, do you have knowledge or facts concerning yourself, your goal, and the Lord that do not really influence your reactions and behavior? It does not matter how many facts you know or how much knowledge and experience you have, if you are still locked into animal reactions. What you have in your mind is *unproductive.*

These are the people who say, "I don't know why he is so successful, or why he got promoted. I know as much as he does, and I have as much experience. It's just not fair! He must know someone or have something on someone."

Probably "he" has moved into human thinking, while the speaker is still operating in animal reactions.

There have been apparently successful non-Christians, of course, people with hardened hearts who yet achieve great business or other successes. Yet they are not successful in biblical terminology, nor according to God's criteria. Only those with changed hearts, who are truly human (re-created with renewed minds), can become "kings" and priests to God, or as some translations say, "a kingdom of priests." (Rev. 1:6.)

A person can be born again, live morally, and be "good," but still have problems with faith and trust in God. That means the heart is hardened in some way toward the things of God. The Pharisees of Jesus' day had "animal" hearts, because the law of Moses had become almost an idol. They believed in living by it and could not be truly human enough to believe in Jesus.

The writer of Hebrews called this "an evil heart of unbelief" and admonished the early Christians not to allow their hearts to remain hardened in any way toward God as the Israelites did during the 40-year sojourn in the wilderness. (Heb. 3:7-12.)

After we are born again and given truly human hearts, how can we get rid of the remainders of animal reactions that are still in our minds, our behaviors, and our attitudes? Simply because we are new spirits, new creatures in Christ, does not mean those learned animal reactions automatically go away — unfortunately!

Most of us are like the Apostle Paul was in his early days as a Christian. We "do what we do not want to do, and do not do what we want to do." (Rom. 7:15.) Those animal reactions have governed our behaviors for too many years to let go of all at once, although we are brand new born-again spirits.

We let go of the animal-like carnality through *choices*, as the quote at the top of this chapter says. Many of those reactions are "programmed" into our behavior because of *choices* we made over the years. God will not override the right to choose, which he made part of a truly human creation. If He were going to do that, He would cause everyone to accept Jesus, because it is not His desire for anyone to go to hell. (2 Pet. 3:9.)

However, He will not override the privilege He built into man of making a choice to accept Jesus, to love God, and to do the right thing. If you want to live according to Jimmy Reader's "3-D Formula for Successful Living," you must make choices every day to override those reactions that are more like animal behavior and train your mind to *think* over every choice and measure it by the Word of God. That formula is:

- Dream big.

- Dare to be more than you thought you ever could be.

- Do all you can with what you have where you are now in order to achieve your fullest potential.[2]

Evangelist Andrew Wommack of Colorado Springs says what you do not consider (think about) is an area in which you are going to be hardened. So begin now to examine every action and reaction in the light of whether it is an animal-like habit or a truly considered choice. Wommack wrote:

You can love God and be carnal, but it will cost you your effectiveness. . . . when you consider something other than Jesus, you deaden yourself to the voice of God, and you open yourself to the voice of the enemy. . . . Some of the old television shows we considered "clean" actually hardened our hearts (toward adultery or various other animal reactions) by taking the seriousness out of (sin).[3] [Interpolations in parentheses are comments by the author of this book.]

"Carnal" means reacting and not thinking, living in unbelief so that you do not believe God's promises to us, and operating at a level far below your "rights" and inheritance as a child of God.

The first step toward moving into "human thinking," then, is to develop a sense of trust.

---

[1]Reader, Jimmy. *Breaking Through to Your Highest Potential*, (Tulsa: Honor Books, 1988), p. 141.

[2]Ibid, back cover.

[3]Wommack, Andrew. *Hardness of Heart/Enemy of Faith*, (Colorado Springs: Andrew Wommack Ministries, Inc., 1991), p. 72.

30

Develop a Sense of Trust

Someone who thinks the world is always cheating him is right — (because) he is missing (or has been cheated of) that wonderful feeling of trust in someone or something.[1]

— Dr. Andrew V. Mason

Anyone who has risen to political prominence, or to a leadership role in business, or even in ministry is in physical danger today from sick and deranged individuals. Also, it always has been true that successful people in any field are in danger from competitors attempting to dethrone them.

Those of great wealth, social prominence, or fame must live today with intensive security precautions around their persons as well as their homes and/or businesses. We live in times when simple trust is being eroded day by day. Children particularly must not trust anyone they do not know — and some of those whom they do know!

Living in this atmosphere, it is not always easy to maintain a trust in others or a trust in God. It is easier to become hardened and simply react to other people. However, trust remains an important spiritual and natural ingredient of leadership.

Saul trusted Samuel in the beginning. He believed the things told him by the prophet which were to happen as signs on his way home from the donkey hunt. (1 Sam. 10:4.) He trusted God when he immediately led warriors into battle at Jabesh-Gilead. Sadly enough, he lost his trust through fear that someone would take his throne.

It does not matter how high a position you have, or how long you live, sooner or later someone else is going to be taking your place or position. All of the fear that Saul got into, all of the worrying he did about being dethroned, all of the times he tried to kill his successor, David, did not keep him from being killed in battle.

Fear is not a defense but rather a hole in your defense, which is trust and faith in God.

None of Saul's distrust was *effective* in any way. It simply:

- cost him a comfortable and happy life and, instead, made him miserable
- cost him a relationship that he might have had with David
- cost him the respect of his son Jonathan
- cost him his relationship with God
- cost him the right to hand down the throne to his posterity
- cost him his life

He would have been much better off to have trusted those around him, trusted David, and trusted God to protect him and his office. The key that Saul did not see is that, as long as he was carrying out the purposes of God, he would not lose his office or his life.

We have talked about fear in earlier chapters, but it does not hurt to mention once again that *fear hinders, fear destroys, and fear kills.* A lack of trust is simply fear of one sort or another: fear of betrayal, fear of loss, fear of failure.

Job was righteous in his generation, yet he had one little area in which he was afraid. That lack of trust that God would take care of his children almost cost him everything. He stopped thinking and reacted in fear, and "the thing he feared" came upon him. (Job 3:25.)

Deal With Fears

You can see, then, that the first step to developing a sense of trust is to deal with the things you fear. Practice making plans and developing organizing skills by taking charge of your steps to maturity. This way, you can accomplish more than one thing at a time:

1. Honestly evaluate your emotional reactions and make a list, in order of importance, of all the things of which you are afraid.

2. Alongside each fear, write down *why* you are afraid.

   Where did this fear begin in your life?

   What caused it?

   Why is it still there?

For example, sometimes unforgiveness of people who have caused us hurt or harm means that the fear of being betrayed or hurt again in that way is part of our mindset.

I have heard of a young man who traced his fear of the dark and of something bad happening to him to a time as a very young boy when an older brother took him to a horror movie. Once he forgave the brother and asked God to heal that hurt, the fear left. It had more or less crippled his life.

3. Look up the references to *fear, trust,* and *doubt* in a good concordance, then study all those scriptures to

find God's ways of dealing with those "animal," negative, or ungodly emotions.

4. Find the promises God made to His children and meditate on them until they are real to you and as much a part of your thinking as the multiplication tables. Fear and doubt will be driven out, and trust and peace will fill your heart and mind.

In other words, as the great spiritual leader and founder of the Christian and Missionary Alliance wrote:

Believe the Bible

There are some who believe the Bible,
And some who believe in part,
And some who trust with a reservation,
And some with all their hearts.
But I know its every promise is firm and
    true always;
It is tried as the precious silver,
And it means just what it says.

It is strange we trust each other,
And only doubt our Lord;
We will take the word of mortals,
And yet distrust His word;
But, oh, what light and glory would shine
    o'er all our days,
If we always would remember that He means
just what He says.[2]

— A. B. Simpson

A sense of trust, however, does not mean being gullible or impractical or believing everyone or everything you hear. However, you can judge what is being said or what you read as to its truth or accuracy without distrusting all other people. For example, simply because some members of the national media are biased against Christians does not mean everything else they report is untrue or that all members of the media are anti-Christian.

It simply means that you must *trust* the Holy Spirit for discernment, keep yourself informed on issues of importance, and know the Bible well enough to have a valid yardstick against which to measure subjective truth.

Being able to trust God and to trust others until they prove untrustworthy develops your self-confidence. It develops your ability to trust yourself. On the other hand, remember that self-confidence is not self-dependence. Self-confidence does not mean no one but you can do things right. That is going full-circle back to fear and lack of trust.

Trust in God builds self-confidence in you.

---

[1]"Trust: the New Ingredient in Management," *Business Week*, July 6, 1981.

[2]Simpson, A. B. *The Speaker's Treasury of 400 Quotable Poems*, compiled by Croft M. Pentz, (Grand Rapids: Zondervan Publishing House, 1963, 1965), p. 13.

31

Self-Confidence Is Not
Self-Dependence

*A person who believes in himself is not going to let
anything keep him from receiving God's best. He is going
to take risks and do whatever is necessary to receive the
best from the Lord.*[1]

— Casey Treat

Self-confidence, by definition, is having a strong belief in
one's self. No successful person ever became that way without
believing in himself, or at least being confident he could do
whatever it was he set out to do. If you are not confident about
your abilities or your potential, you are on a shaky foundation
that stress will cause to crumble.

The more you know yourself and know your field, the
more confidence you will develop. However, never get so self-
confident that you lose your sense of dependency on Someone
higher than yourself. With God, you can do all things (or
anything He calls you to do); without God, only those things
are possible that can be done through natural means.

The Amplified Bible translates Philippians 4:13 this way:
I am self-sufficient in Christ's sufficiency. As Christians,

our self-confidence must be based on being in the center of His will and knowing who we are *in* Him.

The Apostle Paul wrote to the Christians at Corinth:

Not that we are sufficient of ourselves to think any thing as of ourselves; but our sufficiency is of God.

2 Corinthians 3:5

With Jesus, Peter had confidence in his ability to walk on water; without Jesus (looking away from Him), Peter lost his self-confidence and his ability to walk on water. At least, he had no self-dependence, but cried out for help when he saw he was sinking. (Matt. 14:29,30.)

Saul was sinking figuratively for a number of years but was too stubborn to cry out for help.

Never get so self-confident that you think you can make it in any field — not even in your personal life — alone. God created mankind as family, not as a group of loners with each "doing his own thing" in his own way. We are a Body of believers, each having his or her place in that Body. (Eph. 4:15.)

Sadly, as with many other things in Saul's life, this principle is illustrated negatively rather than positively. From beginning in fear, Saul developed so much self-confidence over the years that he began to think he could be self-dependent. He forgot who put him where he was. He forgot who made him king. He forgot that he was ruling *for* God and not for himself.

Although we are talking primarily about a Christian becoming a successful leader in his or her chosen field, these principles are true of every successful leader.

Confidence in your ability to do something or to handle something does not mean you can depend only on yourself or that you can go through life without "a little help from your friends."

The Self-Confident Do What Needs To Be Done

The kindergarten story of the "little red hen" who asked for help, did not receive it from any of the others in the farmyard, and went ahead and did things herself is not about self-dependence. It is about doing the right thing in spite of everyone around you refusing to help. She was self-confident, not self-dependent.

If you seek help from others and do not receive it, then self-confidence comes into play. A successful person will do what has to be done, whether or not he has help.

Without Samuel, Saul would never have been king.

Without the servant, Saul never would have found Samuel.

Without brave soldiers, Saul never would have freed Israel from bondage to the Philistines and the other Canaanite tribes who were oppressing them.

Without David, whom he later feared, hated, and tried to kill, Saul and Israel would not have beaten the Philistine champion, Goliath, and won that battle. (1 Sam. 17:41-54.)

Saul's downfall was his independent spirit, his attitude of self-dependency.

A self-confident person is at peace with himself, at peace with God, and at peace with those around him in so far as is possible.

A self-reliant person counts first on his own abilities, is not "wimpy," and looks for assistance only as a last resource.

A self-dependent person thinks no one can do anything as well as he can.

Lack of trust began in the Garden of Eden, and the birth of self-dependence also was in that garden. Read the first three chapters of Genesis, and you will see who encouraged trust in

God. You will see that self-dependence, being "independent" of God the Creator, was instigated by "that old serpent," our adversary, the devil.

Dr. Robert Schuller has written:

God's ultimate objective is to turn you and me into self-confident persons.[2]

Self-confidence is an attitude; it is trust in yourself and, for a Christian, it is based on trust in God. There is an old saying which applies here: *Attitude rather than aptitude will determine your altitude.* Belief in yourself is a greater impetus to success than a great IQ, education, social status, or wealth.

Self-confident people set realistic goals, not just ultimate goals, or places they want to end up, but landmarks along the way.Plan how to get where you want to go in short periods of time, from next month to next year to five years. Then be flexible enough to readjust those if they turn out not to be precisely accurate.

Above all, do not scale down your expectations, but you may need to adjust for new developments. You may need to factor into your equation some new methods, new technologies, and new ideas. Never, however, lose sight of that ultimate goal toward which you are moving.

It helps to understand that God "never promised us a rose garden" after the fall of Adam and Eve. Instead, He warned that we were in for some hard times, some hard work, and some attacks by the enemy in the form of trials and temptations. (Gen. 3:17-19.)

It helps to understand that we must conquer in this earth life or be conquered, but that Jesus already won the war. Therefore, we can have success. We can have victory. We can achieve the purpose God has set before us, both as individuals and as part of the corporate Body of Christ.

We are "more than conquerors," according to the One who made us — and He ought to know.

[1]Treat, Casey. *Blueprint for Life*, (Tulsa: Harrison House, 1989), p. 23.
[2]Schuller, Dr. Robert. *Self-Esteem: The New Reformation*, (Waco, TX: Word Books, 1982), p. 80.

32

You Must Conquer or Be Conquered

The great difference between the real (conqueror in life) and the pretender is, that the one sees into the future, while the other regards only the present; the one lives by the day, and acts on expediency; the other acts on enduring principles and for immortality.[1]

– Edmund Burke

In the 15th chapter of 1 Samuel is the story of God's command to Saul to totally destroy the tribe of the Amalekites with all their possessions. Saul failed to carry out those orders, sparing the best of the spoils as well as the king, Agag.

At the end of his life, believing himself mortally wounded, he tried to commit suicide to avoid the dishonor of being taken by the enemy. He failed at the attempt and failed to talk his armor bearer into doing it for him. In the end, it was an Amalekite who killed Saul. (2 Sam. 1:9,10.)

We might see this as poetic justice. However, it is not an immutable law of God that anything we fail to overcome will overcome us. On the other hand, it does seem that life almost

The Making of a King

always works out that way, no matter in what area this situation arises.

Of course, what Saul really failed to conquer was his self-dependency, his reliance on his own abilities, and in the end, he found that his self-dependency was not justified. You can see, then, that the first place anyone must begin to be a conqueror is over himself.

Overcomers Begin With Themselves

No runner ever won a race without self-control and self-discipline.

No fighter ever won a bout without first conquering himself in the area of training mind and body. We can see from the lives of champions, however, that some of them did not conquer self in other areas of life other than the sports arena, or the boxing ring.

No winner of gold medals ever got them overnight. Winning in any area of life comes by steady, little by little increments of improvement. When you do gain the prize, the same conquering of self must continue in order to remain a winner.

No hero has remained a hero, no champion has remained champion, no successful person has remained successful if there were areas in their lives that had remained unconquered. However, we have the words of many overcomers to cheer us on, people who have learned these principles in their own lives.

First, there are the overcomers in the Bible: Abraham, Isaac, Jacob, Moses, Joshua, Gideon, and on down to the apostles and the believers of the Early Church. Then we have great examples in our own time of courage and determination to overcome, even in what seemed impossible situations.

180

Winston Churchill, in the face of what appeared to be certain defeat of Great Britain by Nazi Germany in 1940, made a number of speeches that heartened the people and raised morale. Britons determined not to be conquered, but to conquer — and they did.

> . . . We shall defend our island, whatever the cost may be, we shall fight on the beaches, we shall fight on the landing grounds, we shall fight in the fields and in the streets, we shall fight in the hills; we shall never surrender . . . .[2]

Then there was the late Rev. Dr. Martin Luther King's "I Have a Dream" speech on August 28, 1963, at the Washington Monument/Lincoln Memorial:

> With this faith we will be able to hew out of the mountain of despair a stone of hope. With this faith we will be able to transform the jangling discords of our nation into a beautiful symphony of brotherhood.[3]

In your personal quest for success, the principle is the same as for nations, companies, and races — conquer what holds you back or be conquered.

Watch Out for the Amalekites

What is *your* big "mountain"?

What must you overcome before it overcomes you? Pride, fear, prejudice, slothfulness, depression, self-will, rebellion, low self-esteem?

All of those things are today's "Amalekites." Destroy whichever one is after you, before it ruins your life. The late Scottish physician-novelist A. J. Cronin, who wrote several famous novels with Christian themes, once wrote:

The virtue of all achievement is *victory over oneself.* Those who know this can never know defeat.[4]

How do we "kill" the Amalekites? We do that the same way Jesus told His disciples to deal with such things.

> **Then Jesus said to his disciples, "If anyone would come after me, he must deny himself and take up his cross and follow me. For whoever wants to save his life will lose it, but whoever loses his life for me will find it.**
>
> **Matthew 16:24,25**

"Denying" oneself daily is "taking up the cross." As Christians, we know that only so much can be accomplished through acts of will. Only with the help of the Holy Spirit can we be more than conquerors.

> **. . . In all these things we are more than conquerors through him who loved us.**
>
> **Romans 8:37**

In all what things are we more than conquerors? Through the worst life can throw at us, including persecution and death, the Apostle Paul wrote to the Romans. We can be winners *because of the love of God* and our faith in Him.

One "Amalekite" that can cause us to be blind to the right path, the right ways, and the right goal is tradition, or custom. Sixteenth-Century French essayist Montaigne once wrote:

> The principal effect of the power of custom (tradition, or the past) is to seize and ensnare us in such a way that it is hardly within our power to get ourselves back out of its grip and return unto ourselves. . . .[5]

The equation of success does not include redundancy. Although an agnostic, Aldous Huxley expressed some very wise insights into the "animal" nature of humans. Also in the foreword to *Brave New World*, he wrote:

Rolling in the muck is not the best way of getting clean.[6]

As I wrote earlier, wallowing in remorse and condemnation only leads to self-pity, not to making a fresh and clean start. Carrying into your future the wrong attitudes and wrong facts of the past are like fastening great weights on your ankles while trying to run a race. Before long, you will find yourself sitting on the sidelines wondering what happened.

Attitudes many times serve as "Amalekites" in our lives. Dealing with them helps us find the right equation for success.

---

[1]*The New Dictionary of Thought*, p. 407.

[2]Bennett, *The Book of Virtues*, "We Shall Fight in the Hills and in the Streets," p. 572; excerpt from Prime Minister Winston Churchill's address to Parliament, June 4, 1940.

[3]Ibid, p. 574.

[4]Cronin, A.J. "Quotable Quotes," *Reader's Digest*, February 1997, p. 49.

[5]Seldes, The *Great Thoughts*, p. 327; Montaigne's *Essays*, Bk. 1, Ch. 23.

[6]Huxley, p. vii.

33
Right Attitudes + Right Facts = Success

It is not what happens to you that really matters in life – it is your perception of what happened, and it is what you do about it that counts.

Many great minds have stated this truth: More important than situations are our reactions to, or perceptions of, those situations. No success has ever been truly achieved without both right attitudes and right facts; however, sometimes attitudes are *more* important than facts.

Saul had the right facts all of his life, but he developed many wrong attitudes. Therefore, although he was king for forty years, he never was truly a successful king, a successful man, or a successful father.

He had only part of the "success equation."

No matter in what area of life your goal is set, the first step on the way to that goal is *the right attitude*. Perhaps I should say "the right attitudes," because having the right attitude in one aspect will not carry you to total success.

Saul had the right attitude toward defeating Israel's enemies, but he never reached his goal of holding the throne for his posterity, because he had wrong attitudes toward God and other people. Apparently, he also had the wrong attitude toward himself.

Paul — the biblical writer who said the most about right attitudes and facts and/or reaching goals and winning the race — wrote to Christians in the Asia Minor city of Ephesus (now in Turkey) the three steps to achieving right attitudes:

> **You were taught, with regard to your former way of life, to *put off your old self*, which is being corrupted by its deceitful desires; *to be made new in the attitude of your minds*; and *to put on the new self*, created to be like God in true righteousness and holiness.**
>
> **Ephesians 4:22,23**

The *old self* is the person you were before being made a new creature in Christ, the person with the "animal" heart full of "Amalekites" (deceitful desires). God receives you as an adopted child with full rights of inheritance when you accept Jesus. However, it is up to you to "put off" the old lifestyle. God will not make your choices for you.

The *attitudes of your mind* that must be made new are the old ways of thinking that caused the old ways of acting. Right facts from the Bible about God, the universe, and yourself must replace the wrong facts instilled by the world's educational, entertainment, and cultural teachings. Those teachings are opposite to God's Word.

The *new self* that you must "put on," according to Paul, are those attitudes that flow out of the new spirit created within you by the Holy Spirit. The attitudes of the new self basically are found in Galatians 5:22-26:

> **But the fruit of the Spirit is love, joy, peace, patience, kindness, goodness, faithfulness, gentleness and**

self-control. Against such things there is no law. Those who belong to Christ Jesus have crucified the sinful nature with its passions and desires. Since we live by the Spirit, let us keep in step with the Spirit. Let us not become conceited, provoking and envying each other.

There is that word again, *crucified*. The sinful nature with its sinful facts and attitudes must be "put to death" by choice in order for your outward personality (your soul) to reflect the inward new nature that is like Jesus.

Learn the Right Facts

Once you have your attitudes straightened out, you will be able to deal with the facts. You will be able to discern between right and wrong facts and to act on the right ones. Walking in the fruit of the Spirit is the best builder of self-esteem that I know about. Self-esteem then leads to self-confidence and knowledge that you must depend on God to gain and maintain victory.

The "right facts" must cover the entire spectrum of life:

- Without the right facts, *your marriage* will not be as successful. With the right attitudes, it may be peaceful and free of strife and contention. If you add right facts about your spouse's wants and needs, and about what marriage is supposed to be, you can gain and maintain a much more fulfilling and satisfying relationship.

- The "right facts" about *your children* will make you a better parent, although the right attitudes will go a long way. The right facts include knowing that each child is a different personality with different needs and different ambitions. Very seldom can two children in the same family be handled the same way.

- The right facts about *your goal in life*, the purpose God has for you, will make all the difference to success, although the right attitudes will allow you to function in any job and to get along with bosses and co-workers. If you are headed toward the wrong goal, however, you will be unsuccessful in life, no matter how much money you make or how high a position you gain.

- The right facts about *your field of endeavor* sometimes can be learned through study of books. Other times, it is trial and error. If you are "breaking new ground," there is no way to get the right facts except by experimenting until you discover them.

True leaders do not mind going down new paths, exploring new territories, and enduring scorn, ridicule, and trouble because of moving contrary to the flow of custom. To use Thomas Edison once again as an example, his curiosity about how things worked got him in "a heap of trouble" before he found the right path.

> When he was six, he burned the family barn to the ground, because he wanted "to see what it would do." His father beat him before a large and enthusiastic crowd in the public square in Milan, Ohio, where Edison was born. . . .

> Humble Midwestern upbringing, lack of formal education, constant poverty, and crushing indebtedness throughout his early life, failed early inventions — none of these stopped, or even significantly slowed, Edison's momentum as an inventor.[1]

Other modern facts which we take for granted were once ridiculed. It was considered a fact in pre-Civil War days that bathing once a day would make you sick, that man could not move faster than 15 miles an hour without doing damage to his brain, and that if God wanted man to fly, He would have created him with wings!

The majority of the science and medicine of past generations consisted of wrong facts. In fact, it is simply God's mercy that more people did not perish because of those wrong facts. For example, it was considered a fact that doctors had no need to wash their hands between patients! I wonder what things we accept as absolute truth today which really are not true at all?

Whether you are in a position to move through the door of opportunity when it opens depends on whether or not you have learned the right facts about God, yourself, and the field in which your goal is set.

Whether or not you can act on those facts and move toward that goal successfully depends on the right attitudes. However, it is not always necessary to burn down the barn to find out how fire works!

Together, facts and attitudes constitute an equation that adds up to success or failure. If you begin now to put off the old nature and put on the new one and to get prepared for opportunity to know, you will have reach a place of readiness for success.

---

[1]Kuechle, Jeff. "You Light Up My Life," *Coast to Coast Magazine*, (Englewood, CO: Coast to Coast Resorts), May, 1997), p. 25. From "The Low Road" column and The Bettman Archive.

34
Adopt the Boy Scout Motto:
Be Prepared

Opportunity is only opportunity to those who are prepared. To others, opportunity is invisible or a quick glimpse of a possibility that is now impossible.

Being prepared simply means being ready for whatever comes next. Doctors, child psychologists, educators, and physical trainers of all types are using the term "readiness" more and more to define a certain stage of preparedness in a person's life.

An individual, a society, or a culture is thought to have to achieve a certain level of maturity before he or it can become fully functioning. A child of any age can be well-prepared to function in his age group. He can function fully among his peers, but not in a group of greater maturity.

The whole philosophy behind education used to be getting individuals prepared at one level to move into the next. Today, the emphasis seems to be on teaching individuals to be happy, or self-satisfied, with where they are.

Nations not prepared to defend themselves usually are conquered or have to struggle much harder to avoid being conquered. It is never as easy to "play catch up" as it is to prepare ahead of time.

The classic, very basic, truth about being prepared is found in Aesop's fable of the ant and the grasshopper. The ant knew that winter was coming and worked very hard to prepare for the time when she could not get out and gather food. The grasshopper only dealt with the present and made no preparation for the future.

When winter came, of course the grasshopper soon became very hungry and cold. The "moral" or last line of the story says:

Then the grasshopper knew it is best to prepare for the days of necessity.[1]

Of course, King Solomon, who lived hundreds of years before Aesop, Greek writer of morality tales in 550 B.C., already had drawn the same lesson from the ant.

Ants are creatures of little strength, yet they store up their food in the summer.

Proverbs 30:25

Taking Chapter 10 of 1 Samuel as a whole, it is interesting to observe that Saul was anointed as king, filled with the Spirit, given a new attitude (heart), given the responsibility of the office, and then separated from his mentor. He was told by Samuel to go to Gilgal and wait seven days for further instructions.

Everyone Has a "Gilgal"

Gilgal is from a root word meaning "rolling" or "to roll," in the sense God used it when He told the Israelites He had "rolled away" the reproach of Egypt from them. (Josh. 5:9.)

The fact that Samuel told Saul to wait there for further instructions had a spiritual significance as well as being a literal location.

God had rolled away from Saul the reproach of being a "nobody" from a nothing family in a tribe that was a nonenity in Israel. By changing Saul's heart (1 Sam. 10:9), God had made him a "somebody."

However, the point Saul overlooked is that God did not do this for Saul because he deserved it or because he wanted it. God did it for His purposes and for the greater good of Israel. If Saul could have remembered this and developed humility, his story would be quite different.

After we are born again, we need to "go to Gilgal" (Bible study and prayer) and await further instructions. Too many people have gone into the right fields headed toward the right goals, but without the right preparation and failed.

For some, "Gilgal" means seminary; for others medical school; for others a different kind of college degree; for others a technical education; for others, service in the military, and for some, simply self-education and research. You must determine the kind of preparation you need to reach your goal and then begin to get prepared.

Dr. Mensa Otabil, pastor of the more than 6,000-member International Gospel Church in Accra, Ghana, has written:

> You must build yourself up and wait for the opportunity to move out. You cannot wait for the opportunity to arrive and then build yourself up. There will not be time. Whether or not you make good use of that opportunity depends on whether you have developed yourself or not. *Be ready when opportunity knocks.* Time spent in development is not time wasted.[2]

Clarence Birdseye, who began the well-known company that helped pioneer frozen foods, was prepared to seize an opportunity when one came along. Working as a naturalist in Labrador, he noticed that meat frozen quickly in 40 below zero weather tasted better than meat frozen more slowly.

Back home, he experimented with quick-freezing a number of foods. In 1929, he sold his frozen food business for $22 million, a very good price for the Depression era![3]

Right attitudes, right facts, and right preparation will enable you to handle things in the right way.

---

[1]"The Ant and the Grasshopper," *Aesop's Fables*.

[2]Otabil, Dr. Mensa. *Four Laws of Productivity*, (Tulsa: Vincom, Inc., 1991), p. 92.

[3]*Encyclopedia of 7700 Illustrations*, p. 1588, #7240.

35
Handle Things
in the Right Way

*Sometimes doing a right thing in a wrong way is as bad
as doing a wrong thing in a right way – or as doing a
wrong thing, period!*

Many incidents in the life of Saul reveal that he was an
impetuous, impulsive, almost flighty type of person who never
developed the knack of handling things in a mature, proper,
and acceptable way. Saul began rightly, getting to what we might
call "the teenage-stage," then refusing to mature into an adult.

His attitude of jealousy and imagined competition with
David is typical teenage behavior. He reacted too much of the
time instead of acting. David exhibited much more mature
behavior and, certainly, more right attitudes.

When Saul offered sacrifices in Samuel's place, although
he offered them in the right way, it was as wrong a thing to do
as sparing the animals God had said to kill. Saul was not only
judged by God but suffered consequences.

On the other hand, when David was bringing the ark back
to Jerusalem after its long sojourn among the Philistines, an

Israelite did the wrong thing out of ignorance, not out of rebellion, and still suffered the consequences of death. Whether he disobeyed out of rebellion or out of ignorance, what God said would happen occurred.

That is what laws and principles are: the stating of irrevocable facts. Do this, and that automatically happens. Jump off a cliff and the law of gravity automatically applies, which means you are going to hit bottom hurt or dead, depending on the height, and so forth. Simply because you do not know that law or even do not agree with it will not stop the results from occurring.

The ark began to fall, and a man named Uzzah reached out and touched it in a reflex action. (1 Chron. 13:9,10.) The Israelites had been told through Moses that it was dangerous for those not anointed as priests to touch the ark of the covenant. It was not to be touched or moved on a cart, but only carried by duly consecrated Levites by poles inserted through rings in the sides of the ark. (Ex. 25:12-15.)

That is simply a fact of spiritual life: the power of the Holy Spirit cannot be touched with impunity by ungodly persons. Even children of God who handle His glory in the wrong way may be in trouble. (Isa. 48:11.)

The principle is true in any area of life, even in the secular world. Someone who goes into a factory and, in ignorance, touches a live wire, will at least be hurt if not killed. Intentions will not protect you, if you do a wrong thing even in the right way.

In the case of moving the ark, after Uzzah died, David stopped right in the middle of the road saying, "How will I ever get this back to Jerusalem?" (1 Chron. 13:12.)

Of course, that is a question he should have asked before starting out. He took the ark to a nearby Israelite house and went back to the city. The next time they went after the ark, instructions from Moses's writings were followed as to how to move it. (1 Chron. 15:11-28.) Then they could do the right thing in the right way.

Careful study and preparation made it possible to execute the operation, in other words. In 1 Chronicles 15:13, David observed:

> ... **We did not inquire of him about how to do it in the prescribed way.**

Another translation says, "We handled the matter improperly."

Not only can it be dangerous not to handle things right, but it offends those around you if this occurs in social situations. The late Wisconsin sociologist Thorsten Veblen once remarked:

> There are few things that so touch us with instinctive revulsion as a breach of decorum.

In a moment of exasperation at Alexander Haig's shoot-from-the-hip style of providing misinformation during the early days of the Reagan Administration, I penned these words: "Purity of purpose proffers no pardon for lack of proper policy and/or procedure for orderly procession."

In other words, good intentions do not excuse improper handling of information, events, and situations. Nor will good intentions protect you from danger, as we have seen. Not handling things right can cost you money, promotion, a job or career, marriage, and last but not least, possibly even your life.

Those starting out along the path to success (the way to their goals) should make up their minds to become mature, thinking adults who are guided by truly human hearts. Mature "kings in training" make sure they are prepared to handle anything that comes up in the right way.

Such preparation will put you in a position to "execute the program" when the program for success comes into view.

36
Execute the Program

What begins in the heart must be carefully cultivated to come to full fruit in action.[1]

— Frank Damazio

It is one thing to create an office or position, put a person in it, and set up the "machinery" and/or procedures for that office; it is another thing for the person set in office to execute the program.

If we could ask the founding fathers of this country to look at how their conceptions of the top offices have been fulfilled, I believe they would be appalled in many cases, not satisfied that their intents have been carried out.

Saul was anointed in a private ceremony (1 Sam. 10:1), and then set in office in a public ceremony. (1 Sam. 10:17-25.) In 1 Samuel 11:14,15, Samuel and the people reconfirmed Saul as king in another public ceremony. As this was the first time Israel had a king, the "mechanics" for crowning kings and for kings to operate had to be set in place.

> **Samuel explained to the people the regulations of the kingship. He wrote them down on a scroll and deposited it before the Lord (in the tabernacle)....**
>
> **1 Samuel 10:25**

After that, it was up to Saul to "execute the program" of kingship. Obviously, Saul skipped the step of getting prepared, because he had no opportunity to do so. On the other hand, David had a number of years to prepare for kingship, first as a leader of men and a fighter of battles. In addition, David spent time at Saul's court observing the lifestyle and attitudes of a king.

Ancient Greeks defined *preparation* as getting something or someone ready to function properly. As we have seen, Saul functioned properly as a leader mostly on the field of battle in the early days. His appearance and even his endorsement by Samuel did not make up for character, self-esteem, and preparation.

Ignoring the hypotheses of evolutionists and makers of modern myths about ancient man, we can start with recorded history and see three kinds of "programs" that mankind in general has had to live and function within:

1. Tribal/small town civilization

2. Industrial society

3. Technological society

Up until the 18th century, little had changed in man's environment in the sense of communication, transportation, and basic materials of which clothes, furniture, and equipment were made. Men were farmers, fishermen, hunters, craftsmen, professionals such as doctors, teachers, attorneys, and scribes (those who wrote letters and kept accounts for wealthier men or for those who could not write).

Fashions changed — but clothes were made by hand from linen, wool, silk, and leather for millennia.

Styles of transportation changed — but people rode in carts or carriages, walked or rode mules, donkeys, or horses from Adam and Eve to the late 1800s.

Labor involved working for oneself or for wealthier men — in houses, fields, and shops using tools made by hand from wood or iron.

It was not difficult to find one's goal in life or to get prepared to achieve it. Unless one were unfortunate enough to become a slave, a serf (in England and Western Europe), or an indentured servant in America's colonial days (one bound for only a certain number of years to a master), there was hard physical labor but not a lot of mental or emotional stress — compared to what that kind of stress means today.

Young men were apprenticed to printers, craftsmen, and other vocations instead of attending "tech" or vocational schools. There was one-on-one training and preparation so that when the time came for the young man to "execute the program" on his own, he was ready to do so.

Almost overnight, with the advent of machines of various kinds, life changed. For the first time in known history, ways of communication, transportation, and making the clothes, tools, and artifacts of life were drastically different. Man had to change to adapt to his changed environment.

"Executing the program" became very, very different from the time of their ancestors. Then in this century, with the invention of television, electronics, and computers, once again life changed drastically. Children in very early grades learn how to operate computers, in preparation for life in a new millennium.

Executing the Program Today Is Much Harder

Our lives today are a complex and intricate inter-working of four things, which actually are the same basic things all those before us have had to deal with: "the Four M's" — mind, matter, mood, and morality. However, our outward environments have changed drastically, making these things much more complicated.

Man is no longer a free, independent agent who can live as he pleases. He must deal with world government, not just local, and also with worldwide travel, communication, and trade, with new diseases and potential warfare.

Mind still tells us what should be done, must be done, and can be done.

Matter is what we have to deal with in the natural world: food, clothing, shelter, tools, machinery, vehicles, weather, and other people.

Mood involves our attitudes and emotions, as well as body-influenced ups and downs.

Morality or ethics has to do with the consequences of the choices we make — based on mental conclusions and moods — concerning the things of matter, or material, in our lives.

For example, Saul's mind said to him, "Who are you to be king? What if the people do not like it and try to kill you?"

Apparently, Saul's mood promptly sank into his boots, and his way of dealing with "matter" was to hide behind the baggage. He did not foresee or deal at all with the consequences of his choice to hide, which made him look more foolish than if he had faced down the sneers and astonishment of his peers.

In a young man's life today, the sequence of decisions might go like this:

- Mind says, "You need an education to get prepared to handle things right and execute the program in your progression toward a goal of becoming a heart specialist."

- Matter says, "That is going to take a lot of money for books, clothes, tuition, housing, and so forth. This path is going to require a lot of work, sacrifice, and time."

- Mood says either, "Go for it!" or "To heck with it. This is too hard. I want a life!"

- Morality, or conscience, says, "What are the consequences of either path? What will my future be like either way? What kind of life can I provide for a wife and children depending on which road I take?"

The basic questions of life remain the same, whether in Saul's simple times or in our complex space age. Two other examples involve individual choices and civic choices:

- Mind says, "I should not ingest these addictive substances. They are bad for me."

- Matter says, "But marijuana is so cheap and so available. People even use it for medicinal purposes. It has not been proven to be bad for you."

- Mood says, "I am depressed, or I'm in pain. I need a lift. Besides, I can't deal with being rejected or made fun of by my friends if I don't. I can't deal with being different."

- Moral function says, "What will this do to my body, in spite of the surveys? What will it do to my mind? I can see from my friends' that pot does affect mind and memories."

Suppose you live in a community that needs a new water plant, or it could be a school, police or fire equipment, or new roads. In the early days of this century, roads were still maintained and constructed in many places by each male citizen donating so many days of his time to work on them. Today, we only worry about how to pay for them! Concerning a new water plant:

- Mind says, "We do need a new water plant, or we may have to live with rationing or water not up to health standards. What if we have another drought this summer?"

- Matter says, "The town has no money to build a new plant, nor any land on which to put it. This means higher taxes."

- Mood says, "I'm tired of bond elections, taxes constantly being raised, and all this worry about water. Maybe we just ought to move somewhere else."

- Moral sense says, "What about my children or my grandchildren? What about the other people who live here with their children?"

There is no way a person can reach his goal in life and achieve his purpose without dealing with the "Four M's." We must plan our lives, then live out our plans. Once you have sorted out all of this in your own life, it is time for you to get up and be on your way.

---

[1]Damazio, Frank. *The Making of a Leader*, (Portland, OR: Bible Temple Publishing, 1988), p. 105.

37
Do What You Know To Do

Good luck is when preparation meets opportunity – or the hardest part of any job is getting started.

The early part of 1 Samuel 10 lists this interesting sequence of events that happened to Saul:

He was chosen and anointed king of Israel

He was given a mission.

He was introduced to the glories of high expectation.

He was taught to trust.

He tasted the power and thrill of operating in a prophetic flow.

He was imbued with the Spirit of the Lord.

However, at that point, the prophet said to him, in essence, "From now on, your decisions should be based on whatever seems best under the circumstances *for the Lord will guide you.*"

It was as if Samuel were telling Saul, "We have laid the foundation, done the homework for you, and made the preparations for the office. Now you are in a position to capitalize on whatever might come your way. From now on, it is up to you to make your own 'luck.'"

Another biblical example of this is found in the time between Joshua and the beginning of Israel having kings, during the 400 years when judges were raised up periodically by God to lead the nation in times of trouble. The governor of a city where a usurper rose against the son of the judge Gideon, wrote to the son in this manner:

> **Now then, during the night you and your men should come and lie in wait in the fields. In the morning at sunrise, advance against the city. When Gaal and his men come out against you, do whatever your hand finds to do."**
>
> **Judges 9:32,33**

In other words, I have helped you with strategy, now it is up to you to make your own luck. Another translation says, "Do to them as occasion offers."

In any situation or circumstances, do you consider what occasion offers? Do you consider that God has helped put you in the right place at the right time, so it is up to you to "make your own luck"? To do what your hand finds to do?

Newspaper advice columnist Ann Landers once wrote that no experience is bad, if it teaches us something good.

That wise writer, Anonymous, once said that both good and bad luck are but synonyms for good and bad judgment, in most cases. Also, he said that luck is a lazy man's opinion of a working man's success.

The late Harry Emerson Fosdick, an American Baptist minister who was a leader in the "Modernist" (whom we would call "liberal" today) movement, said it best as far as the author of this book is concerned (although I disagree with his theology):

For one thing, to suppose that a dangerous situation must issue in fearfulness, self-pity, and panic is to misread human nature. Peril *can* be a great stimulant. Put one man into a perilous situation, and he is scared stiff. Put another man into the same situation, and he is aroused (to action) by the stimulus. Peril pulls the trigger, but what it explodes depends on what a man is loaded with. One man responds with nervous collapse, consternation, and frightened weakness. Another man responds with realized energies and a stimulated mind.

No matter how it is said, the message is the same: Good or bad, happy or sad, triumphant or traumatic — what any occasion offers is strictly in terms of one's response to it. Here is what *occasion* can offer:

- An opportunity to believe the promises of God
- A challenge to talent and inspiration
- A change of direction, a new start
- An "alternator" (charger) for new life
- A opening to new sociability, meeting new friends
- An opportunity to analyze one's life, one's behavior and attitudes, and one's goals
- A reminder of responsibility or obligation.

Those Who Have Done What Occasion Offered

Clarence Birdseye, the frozen foods pioneer mentioned in an earlier chapter, made his own luck when he observed an interesting fact in Labrador. Some would not have noticed the difference in taste between quick and slow frozen foods. Others would have noted it as an interesting fact — perhaps many others had done just that. This man seized the occasion and began an entirely new career and new life.

Another man, U.S. Gen. Robert Wood, retired from military service but not from life. Accepting retirement as a challenge, not an end, he joined Montgomery Ward's as vice president. Asked to resign because he had too many "radical" ideas of how to improve the company, he accepted "failure" as just another opportunity.

Joining Sears as vice president, he was given free rein. As chairman of the board, the late Wood was responsible for most of the growth of Sears after World War I.[1]

He never stopped studying and learning, even reading U.S. census reports once for lack of other reading material. That triggered the understanding that the automobile was changing the face of American society. The "occasion" offered the idea of this mail-order company building retail stores for the first time, particularly in the South and West along the growing network of highways.

The perils of the stockmarket crash in 1929 did not faze him in the least. He saw a challenge in increased auto traffic with its accompanying danger of accidents and urged Sears to start a vehicle insurance company, selling its policies by mail. At first, his fellow executives thought he was crazy, but finally went along with him. Thus Allstate Insurance Co. was born.

Possibly one of the few all-around examples of men whose lives show the principles in this book, Wood not only saw needs and met them, but he never lost an opportunity to encourage other people and build them up. He had a human heart.

> Though he always had about him the crusty air of the old calvaryman, he was, underneath, as soft as the caramels he popped into his mouth. . . . He had an incredible memory for names and faces, and

often amazed employees he had met once long before by asking about their children by name.[2]

In more recent times, Scott McGregor's family sacrificed greatly for him to work on his "invention," once being within two days of eviction from their home. Yet today, his firm, Telemac Cellular Corp., is an industry leader in phone computer chips that will make a billing record of each call, not possible before McGregor's break-through.[3]

President Theodore Roosevelt wrote:

A life of ignoble ease, a life of that peace which springs merely from lack either of desire or of power to strive after great things, is as little worthy of a nation as of an individual. . . . We admire the man who embodies victorious effort; the man who never wrongs his neighbor; who is prompt to help a friend; but who has those virile qualities necessary to win in the stern strife of actual life.[4]

Do what you know to do, and you can expect results strictly in proportion to the effort you have put forth.

[1]Reddy, John. "The General Who Built the World's Largest Store," *Discovery, The Allstate Motor Club Magazine*, Winter 1964, (Skokie, IL: Allstate Enterprises, 1963); condensed in *Reader's Digest*, January 1964, pp. 181-185.

[2]Ibid, pp. 182,183.

[3]McConnell, Malcolm. "They Dared to Dream," *Reader's Digest*, June 1996, pp. 109,110.

[4]Roosevelt, Theodore. "In Praise of the Strenuous Life," *The Book of Virtues*, p. 416.

38

Expect Results in Proportion to Effort

The woodchuck never tired of telling all about, "I'm going to build a dwelling six stories high, up to the sky." He dug the cellar smooth and well, but made no more advances, for that lovely hole so pleased his soul and satisfied his fancies.[1]

The woodchuck in the little poem never got a finished building, because he was satisfied with the hole dug for the foundation. He got results in proportion to his efforts. So will you.

When King Saul was securely "in the saddle" as leader of the nation, he immediately began to build an army for Israel out of farmers, woodsmen, and small craftsmen whose work tools had to double for implements of war. The Philistines had made blacksmithing illegal, so that the Israelites even had to go to their enemies to get their hoes and plowshares made and sharpened. (1 Sam. 13:19-21.)

Saul did what "occasion offered," however, and with the Lord's help, the Israelites took the armament they needed as they overthrew the surrounding tribes. The Philistines,

Moabites, Ammonites, Edomites, and others soon learned it was a new day! Wherever Saul turned, he was successful. He did great deeds and conquered enemies. (1 Sam. 14:46-48.) He worked at what he knew to do, seized the initiative, and achieved results commensurate with his efforts.

The late President Theodore Roosevelt wrote:

It is hard to fail; but it is worse never to have tried to succeed. In this life we get nothing save by effort. A man can be freed from the necessity of work only by the fact that he or his fathers before him (already) have worked to good purpose. . . . But if he treats this period of freedom from the need of actual labor as a period *not of preparation* but of enjoyment, he shows that he is a mere cumberer on the earth's surface . . . . A mere life of ease is not in the end a satisfactory life.[2]

Do you want to be "a mere cumberer," or hindrance, on earth?

Do you resent, dread, or dodge work to one degree or another? If so, you need to re-read the first chapters of Genesis. God created man with work built into his make-up. Work was to occupy the majority of man's time — six days as opposed to one day of rest, which day was to remember and worship God, not just to rest man's body.

The difference in man and his environment after the Garden of Eden fiasco is what caused "work" to be hard and drudgery, not fulfilling and a pleasure. Those who are slothful or want to "live in flowery beds of ease" never know the satisfaction of completing a task or the fulfillment of knowing a job was done well.

Work is a "four-letter" word, but not a dirty word to be avoided.

Work is something to be looked forward to, not dreaded.

Work is necessary and desirable.

Sir James M. Barrie (British author of *Peter Pan* and other books and plays) defined work this way:

Nothing is really work unless you would rather be doing something else.[3]

Blessings Follow Effort

Blessings of God will not fall on you no matter what you do, although they cannot be "earned," in the ordinary sense of the word.

Blessings fall on you *because* of *what* you do (in God's purpose for you), *how* you do it (with a good heart), *when* you do it (in the right timing), *why* you do it (with the right attitude), and *where* you do it (in God's will).

The ancient Israelites and Christians, the children of Abraham by faith (Gal. 3:29), alike were and are blessed because of hearing and obeying, not because of sitting on the front porch rocking when the crops are withering on the vine. (Deut. 28:1-14.)

The subject of work, or effort, has elicited comments from some of the wisest men in history:[4]

- A man is a worker; if he is not that, he is nothing. (Joseph Conrad)

- Men do not break down from overwork, but from worry and dissipation. (Charles E. Hughes)

- I never did anything worth doing by accident, nor did any of my inventions come by accident. (Thomas A. Edison)

- Work is as much a necessity for man as eating and sleeping. (W. Humboldt)

The writer of Ecclesiastes, whom most scholars believe to be King Solomon, wrote that accepting one's lot and being happy in one's work is "a gift from God." (Eccl. 5:19.) The man who accepts that one's lot in life is to work:

... Seldom reflects on the days of his life, because God keeps him occupied with gladness of heart.

Ecclesiastes 5:20

In 2 Kings 13:14-19, an incident from the life of Elisha, a prophet long after Samuel's time in the reign of a much-later king of Judah, illustrates perfectly that you get the results of what you do.

King Jehoash visited Elisha as he lay dying and was lamenting about what the country would do without this great "defender of Israel." The prophet told the king to get his bow and arrows, then placing his hand on the king's hand, he instructed him to open the window facing toward Israel's enemy, Syria.

Elisha then said, "Shoot the arrow!"

The king did so and was told prophetically that *he* was the Lord's arrow with which God would win the victory over Syria. However, even at such a dramatic time as the death of a great prophet and even with having heard such a great prophecy concerning himself, the king was hesitant to strike the ground with his other arrows, as Elisha ordered.

His hesitancy or his slothfulness — or whatever motivated this king to be slack instead of zealous and diligent — cost him the complete victory.

To work hard without laying the foundation suggested by the earlier principles is the same as "striking the ground" two or three times instead of five or six. Hard work will yield only minimal results without the proper foundation.

On the other hand, to do all the others and not work hard will yield negative results — high hopes and expectations will end in complete disillusionment.

You must have high expectations of reaching a goal; you must have the proper preparation of spirit, soul, and body; and you must then work as hard as necessary to accomplish the thing for which you have laid the foundation.

[1]L.J. Bridgman. *The World's Greatest Literature*, Vol 20, p. 7055. (New York: Standard Reference Works Pub. Co., Inc., 1958).

[2]*The Book of Virtues*, p. 417.

[3]*The New Dictionary of Thoughts*, "Work," p. 741.

[4]Ibid, pp. 740-742.

39
Expectation, Preparation, and Work Make a "King"

The Reformation not only overturned dead religion but 1,000 years of thinking that "poverty is next to godliness." Through the efforts of theologian John Calvin, work again became respectable and desirable for all – not just for slaves and servants.[1]

Not a single step or principle outlined in this book can be left out of your planning or preparation without limiting or crippling your achievements. It is a tough discipline, but it will work.

Harold J. Laske aptly sums up my thinking this way:

The test, surely, of a creed is not the ability of those who accept it to announce their faith; its test is its ability to change their behavior in the ordinary round of daily life.[2]

The "creed" or beliefs about success seen in the life of Saul *did* change this author's life. The distilled wisdom of those principles can be expressed like this:

- Know God.

- Know your vision, purpose, and plan of achievement.

- Know yourself, your present ability, and future potential.

- Know your field of endeavor.

- Know the abilities and capabilities, needs and aspirations of those with whom you come in contact — especially those for whom you work and who work with you.

- Know that planning and preparation will go nowhere without effort.

Dr. Thomas Stanley, coauthor of *The Millionaire Next Door*, has found that most of today's millionaires made their money and did not inherit it. He says they made their fortunes by hard work, planning ahead, sticking to that plan (or goal), being careful with what they have, and by being self-disciplined.[3]

Part of being successful is saving for a rainy day. Even if your salary increases every year but you spend it all, you are simply living better, not getting richer. Stanley's survey showed that most millionaires live in the same homes for years and do not live in lavish homes, but fairly ordinary ones.

They do not wear Rolexes, but watches of less than $300. They are not misers, nor do they deprive themselves. However, they are careful with their resources, not wasteful.

However, the principles in this book are not just for those wanting to become millionaires. They are also for those wanting to successfully complete their purposes in life, for those who want to have enough for their own needs and enough to give to the Lord's work.

No roadblock should stop a child of God from achieving his or her goal. There is always a way to get around, under, or over obstacles.

Many times, I have observed someone who could have achieved his goal if he had kept trying just a little longer. The "rope" of success was dangling out there at the end of his outstretched fingers, but he became so tired and discouraged that he simply quit trying to grasp it.

If he had made a lunge for it or tried once more, he would have had success. The critical point is to *keep God in charge of your affairs*. No one can be strong, vital, or heroic without the presence of the Holy Spirit. The Bible says not to let yourself get "weary in well-doing." (Gal. 6:9.)

There is an old poem that should be the motto of anyone aspiring to success in any field, from business to ministry:

'Tis a lesson you should heed, try, try again;
If at first, you don't succeed, try, try again;
Then your courage should appear; for, if you will
    persevere,
You will conquer, never fear, try, try again. . . .
If we strive, 'tis no disgrace though we do not
    win the race;
What should you do in that case? Try, try again.
Time will bring you your reward, try, try again.
All that other folks can do, why, with patience,
    should not you?
Only keep this rule in view: Try, try again.[4]

So if you have tried and failed — get up and try again! Learn from Saul's good points and his shortcomings. It is not over until it's over!

One of my favorite stories involves an old country preacher, who visited the city for the first time and was compelled by events to remain there over the weekend. As he had never missed church in his life, he dressed on Sunday morning and went out hunting a place to fellowship with the saints and worship God.

Although somewhat scared, lost, and on foot, he began walking with the thought that he would attend the first church to which he came. This happened to be an Episcopal church where the congregation was participating in "high mass" with all of its rituals.

At first, he was embarrassed. Then he decided to watch the man next to him and do what he did. This went along fine in the beginning, but then the service got ahead of him. He found himself sitting down when everyone else was standing up and standing up when the rest were sitting down.

He looked at the man whom he was trying to follow, laughed quietly, and said, "Doesn't this beat the devil?"

The staid old Episcopalian looked back at him thoughtfully and said, "Well, that's the general idea — yeah!"

The "general idea" of this book is: Get prepared to do what occasion offers, make your own "good luck," and work "to beat the devil." Only then can one become a "king."

---

[1]Theme of a book by Jeremy Rifkin with Ted Howard. *The Emerging Order, God in the Age of Scarcity,* (New York: G. P. Putnam's Sons. Copyright 1979 by the two authors.)

[2]Laske, Harold.

[3]Stanley, Dr. Thomas. "How To Become a Millionaire," *Bottom Line/ Personal,* (New York:Long Street Press, 1996).

[4]*Oxford Dictionary of Quotations,* p. 251, #1; quote from the poem, "Try and Try Again," by W. E. Hickson (1803-1870).

About the Author

Tom Leding is a distinguished businessman, broadcaster, and author who has touched the lives of thousands around the world with his motivational messages for success in life.

Tom earned bachelor's degrees in accounting and law from the Oklahoma School of Business and LaSalle University, plus a master's degree in business administration from Golden State University. Additional years of study paid off with a doctorate from the University of Hawaii.

He was chief accountant at American Airlines for nearly five years.

For twenty-three years he was an agent with the Farmer's Insurance Group, where he set company records for the largest single policy ever sold as well as monthly and annual sales marks. For seven years he was Number One among the company's fourteen thousand agents.

Today, Tom has a staff of brokers working in his full-service insurance and investment agency in Tulsa, Oklahoma, while he personally manages a multimillion dollar portfolio for his clients.

His daily radio broadcasts called, "Who Said That?" inspire listeners to reach beyond their present circumstances to be the best they can be. He has made numerous television appearances and also is in demand as a motivational speaker.

Called the "Man With the Midas Touch" by *Voice Magazine*, Tom is the author of the bestselling books, *Wisdom for Success in Life, Rags to Riches: You Don't Have To Be Poor, The Making of a King,* and *The Leding Action Plan for Success.*

A member of the Full Gospel Business Men's Fellowship since 1955, Tom is International Treasurer of the fellowship, which has more than 4,000 chapters in 150 nations. He also has served on the boards of Kenneth Hagin Ministries, Youth for Christ and other ministries.

Tom and his wife, Sue, have one son, Ron, and two grandchildren.

Books by Tom Leding

Wisdom for Success in Life

Rags to Riches: You Don't Have To Be Poor

The Leding Action Plan for Success

The Making of a King:
You Can Rise Above Your Circumstances

To order, call:

1-800-880-8220

Or write to:

TLM Publishing
4412 S. Harvard
Tulsa, OK 74135